ROCKY MOUNTAIN

A Visitor's Companion

George Wuerthner

Photographs by George Wuerthner
Illustrations by Douglas W. Moore

STACKPOLE
BOOKS

Published by
STACKPOLE BOOKS
5067 Ritter Road
Mechanicsburg, PA 17055
www.stackpolebooks.com

Printed in China

Cover design by Caroline M. Stover
Cover photo by George Wuerthner

10 9 8 7 6 5 4 3 2 1

First edition

Library of Congress Cataloging-in-Publication Data

Wuerthner, George.
    Rocky Mountain : a visitor's companion / George Wuerthner ;
photographs by George Wuerthner ; illustrations by Douglas W.
Moore—1st ed.
      p. cm.
    ISBN 0-8117-2919-2
    1. Rocky Mountain National Park (Colo.)—Guidebooks.
I. Title.

F782.R59 W84 2001
917.88'690434—dc21
                                     00-044653

CONTENTS

About the Author

George Wuerthner is a full-time freelance photographer, writer, and ecologist. An authority on national parks and conservation issues, he has written more than twenty other books, including *Yellowstone: A Visitor's Companion, Yosemite: A Visitor's Companion, Grand Canyon: A Visitor's Companion, Olympic: A Visitor's Companion, Texas's Big Bend Country, California Wilderness Areas: Coasts and Mountains, Alaska Mountain Ranges,* and *The Adirondacks: Forever Wild.*

Wuerthner graduated from the University of Montana with degrees in wildlife biology and botany and received a master's degree in science communication from the University of California, Santa Cruz. He spent three additional years pursuing a graduate degree in geography at the University of Oregon. He has worked as a university instructor, wilderness guide, park ranger, and biologist. Wuerthner currently lives in Livingston, Montana, north of Yellowstone National Park.

INTRODUCTION

Rocky Mountain National Park now encompasses 265,726 acres. Compared with other national parks, such as the 3.4 million-acre Death Valley National Park, Rocky Mountain National Park (RMNP) is not particularly large. Nevertheless, it contains one of the most spectacular segments of what geographers call the Southern Rocky Mountains. The park includes a twenty-five-mile stretch of the Continental Divide and is bounded on the west by the Kawuneeche Valley and Never Summer Range and the community of Grand Lake, while the eastern slope is defined by the community of Estes Park and Highway 7. The park lies just a two-hour drive northwest of Denver and less than an hour from Fort Collins, Loveland, and Boulder.

Ranging from 7,800 to 14,225 feet, the park contains representative examples of all the major vegetation communities found in the central Rockies, including one of the most expansive examples of alpine tundra in the United States. Though Rocky Mountain National Park is high and mountainous, it is still surprisingly sunny and characterized by mild winters and pleasant summers.

All of the lands in the Estes Park region, both the park and national forests, are located within the Southern Rockies bioregion. This bioregion includes the Medicine Bow and Laramie Ranges in Wyoming, all of Colorado's mountains, and a few ranges in northern New Mexico, including the Jemez Mountains and Sangre de Cristo Range. For the most part, these mountains are aligned in a north-south orientation, with the 180-mile-long Front Range, which includes Rocky Mountain National Park, one of the longest ranges in the chain. Here the Continental Divide reaches its easternmost position in North America. Rising dramatically from the Great Plains, the Front Range is one of the longest mountain ranges in the West and makes up the bulk of Rocky Mountain National

Never Summer Range, along the western boundary of Rocky Mountain National Park.

Park. In addition to the Front Range, the western boundary of the park encompasses the Never Summer Range, a small but spectacular mountain range west of the Colorado River. The Front Range straddles the Continental Divide, with waters flowing west via the Colorado River drainage and east to the Mississippi via the Big Thompson and North St. Vrain Rivers, tributaries of the Platte River.

The Front Range begins along the Arkansas River near Pueblo and runs north into Wyoming, where it splits into two segments, the Medicine Bow Range and Laramie Range. To the east lie the Denver Basin and the Great Plains, while three large intermontane valleys—North Park, Middle Park, and South Park—border the range on the west.

The Southern Rockies are easily the rooftop of America, with 900 peaks that rise above 11,000 feet and 54 that exceed 14,000 feet. No place outside of Alaska is the land so consistently high—indeed, from Milner Pass in Rocky Mountain National Park to the New Mexico border, there's not one pass on the Continental Divide below 10,000 feet. As the highest point on the Continental Divide, it's not surprising that the Southern Rockies are the headwaters for many of the nation's major rivers, including the North and South Platte, the Arkansas, the Rio Grande, and the mighty Colorado. Two of these, the South Platte and the Colorado, have their headwaters in Rocky Mountain National Park.

Despite the overall height of the Southern Rockies, there is only one 14,000-foot-plus peak in Rocky Mountain National Park: 14,255-foot Longs Peak. In fact, Longs Peak is the only fourteener north of I-70 in Colorado. Nevertheless, a great deal of the park is high terrain; more than a third of the park is above timberline, with 133 peaks rising above 10,000 feet. Sixteen of these peaks exceed 13,000 feet, and 30 are over 12,000 feet. About 98 named peaks poke above 11,000 feet. And the lowest part of the park, at an elevation of 7,522 feet, is still 838 feet higher than Mount Mitchell in the southern Appalachian Mountains—the highest point east of the Mississippi.

Rocky Mountain National Park contains some of the most exten-sive alpine tundra found in any national park, plus more than 150 lakes, lovely meadows, aspen groves, and beautiful subalpine forests cloaking its slopes. Few areas are as good a representation of the Southern Rockies as Rocky Mountain National Park. It's a wonderful place for people new to the Rockies to get a good introduction to the region and a fine place for old hands to enjoy.

National parks are usually managed to maintain native species and ecosystems, and to protect important historic and cultural sites. Com-patible recreational activities are permitted in national parks, including nature study, camping, hiking, mountain climbing, cross-country skiing, and fishing. Due to their restricted management scheme, national parks are biological baselines against which the rest of the landscape can be measured, the majority of which is managed for human exploitative uses. In recognition of its importance, Rocky Mountain National Park was named as the twenty-first Biosphere Reserve in 1976 under the United Nations UNESCO Man and the Biosphere Program, which recognizes landscapes of global significance. According to UNESCO, a Biosphere Reserve "provides a standard against which the effects of man's impact on his environment can be measured."

The park was originally carved from preexisting federal lands and is still surrounded by several national forests and state lands. On the east and north lies the Roosevelt National Forest, to the southwest is the Arapaho National Forest, and directly west of the Never Summer Range is the Routt National Forest. National forests are federally administered lands that differ from national parks in several major ways. Unlike national parks, national forests permit resource extraction industries such

Sawtooth Mountain, Front Range, Indian Peaks Wilderness, Roosevelt National Forest. Rocky Mountain National Park is surrounded by national forest lands that are managed under a multiple-use policy, permitting extractive commercial uses such as logging, livestock grazing, and mining—activities not normally permitted in a national park.

as logging, livestock grazing, mining, and oil and gas development. In addition, hunting is allowed on national forests, while it is generally prohibited in national parks. Some of these national forest lands have special designations. For example, the land surrounding Lake Granby and Shadow Mountain Lake are national forest but also part of the Arapaho National Recreation Area.

Some of the surrounding national forest is also managed as federally protected wilderness, including the Neota Wilderness, Indian Peaks Wilderness, Never Summer Wilderness, and Comanche Peak Wilderness. Wilderness areas are closed to motorized vehicles and most extractive uses, such as logging, mining, and oil and gas development. Unfortunately, however, livestock grazing is permitted in wilderness where it existed prior to establishment of the wilderness area. Recreational uses such as camping, hiking, fishing, and hunting are all permitted in wilderness areas. Nevertheless, these surrounding wilderness areas help expand upon and buffer the protected lands represented in Rocky Mountain National Park.

CLIMATE AND WEATHER

Rocky Mountain National Park has one of the most invigorating and equable climates found in the United States. An abundance of sunshine, winters with moderately cold nights and bright, sunny days, and summers with pleasant daytime temperatures and cool nights create ideal conditions for outdoor physical activity.

It is, on average, considerably colder west of the Divide. Granby sits in Middle Park, a mountain valley where cold air collects, while Estes Park is more open, permitting colder air to move out of the basin. In Granby, frost is a common occurrence, even in summer.

The record high for Estes Park is a mere 90 degrees F, while that for Granby, on the west slope of the Front Range five miles from Grand Lake, is 88 degrees. The record lows are more extreme, due to the occasional influx of frigid arctic air. For example, –39 degrees F has been recorded for Estes Park, while Granby once experienced –41 degrees. Such extremes, however, belie the fact that most winters are extremely mild by comparison to more northerly locations, such as North Dakota or Minnesota. For instance, the average January high in Estes Park is 38 degrees F, while Granby is considerably cooler, at 28 degrees. By comparison, the average January temperature for New York City, at sea level, is approximately the same as at Estes Park.

As a review of the weather differences between Grand Lake and Estes Park reveals, the western slope of the Continental Divide tends to be wetter, and precipitation is more evenly distributed throughout the year. Grand Lake gets twenty inches of precipitation annually to Estes Park's thirteen inches.

These figures tell us something about the climate of the park. Climate is the long-term record of average atmospheric conditions. It has a tremendous influence upon what plants and animals grow in any area, as well as the biological and physical processes that operate in a region. For

Mummy Range in winter. Snowfall east of the Continental Divide near Estes Park is relatively light, with most of the snowfall occurring on the western slope.

example, forest fires are fairly common in Rocky Mountain National Park because lightning from summer thunderstorms is a relatively frequent occurrence. Weather, on the other hand, refers to the day-to-day changes that occur in any particular area.

Two major factors influence the climate and weather of Rocky Mountain National Park: its topographical terrain and its inland location. The Front Range is a formidable barrier to the movement of air masses. The mountainous terrain results in considerable variation in temperature, precipitation, wind, aspect, slope, and other factors that create microclimatic conditions over very small distances. It may be snowing on Trail Ridge while the residents of Estes Park are basking in warm sunshine.

The inland continental location results in dramatic seasonal changes in weather as well as great diurnal variability. The generally arid conditions, with an abundance of sunshine along with low humidity, are the result of the park's distance from oceans as well as the influence of intervening mountains that wring much of the available moisture from air masses before they reach the Front Range.

Rocky Mountain National Park is generally influenced by two major air masses: maritime air masses from the Pacific Ocean or Gulf of Mexico, which tend to contain high amounts of moisture, and continental air masses that originate from the interior of the continent, often from the north, and thus tend to be cold and dry.

The biggest storms and prolonged periods of inclement weather occur in the winter months, when the temperature gradient between the poles and equator is increased, which heightens the velocity of high-elevation winds. This, in turn, enables storm air masses from the oceans to penetrate deeper into the interior of the continent to reach places like Rocky Mountain National Park.

Shifting high-altitude winds known as the jet stream influence the major cyclonic storm tracks. The jet stream generally flows west from the Pacific Ocean and moves across the northern United States and Canada, bringing clouds and moisture along its path. In winter, the jet stream shifts southward toward the U.S.–Canada border, hauling storm after storm across Washington, northern Idaho, Montana, and into the Midwest. Most of these storms miss Colorado. Occasionally, however, a storm track bearing moist maritime air masses is deflected far enough south to drop significant snowfall in northern Colorado, but by the time these storms reach the Front Range, they typically have lost most of their moisture, and the amount of snowfall that occurs here is relatively light.

The largest winter snowfall doesn't usually originate in the Pacific Ocean. There are too many intervening mountains that wring out most of the moisture before air masses arrive at Colorado's Front Range. Rather, the biggest snow-producing storms come from the Gulf of Mexico. Originating over the warm Gulf, these air masses tend to carry a lot of moisture. If this warm air happens to collide with a cold blast of arctic air from the northern plains, as sometimes occurs, blizzardlike conditions occur up and down the mountain front. Some of the deepest snowfall of the winter occurs during these storms. Often during upslope precipitation, the Continental Divide remains as a barrier; it may be a blizzard whiteout on the east slope, while people in Grand Lake are enjoying sunny, dry weather.

Because of the great elevation of the Front Range, combined with the great barometric pressure differences between the lofty peaks and the nearby plains, high winds are frequent, particularly during the winter months. Record winds of 170 miles per hour have been recorded on Trail Ridge Road, and a blast of 201 miles per hour was once clocked on Longs Peak. The U.S. Weather Bureau defines a hurricane as a tropical storm with winds of 74 miles per hour or more. Hurricane-force winds are a regular feature of Rocky Mountain National Park in winter.

Summer brings a northward shift in the jet stream and a weakening of midlatitude westerlies. Much of the time, the air masses passing over Rocky Mountain National Park originate in the dry interior of Nevada and Utah, bringing stable, dry conditions. The abundant sunshine contributes to a pleasant average summertime daily high of 75 degrees F at Grand Lake near the southwest entrance to the park. Due to low humidity, the overall climate is not oppressive but is very conducive to outdoor activities.

On occasion, moist air masses from the Gulf of Mexico drive inland, bringing afternoon thunderstorms to Colorado's mountains. Typically, southern Colorado mountains, like the San Juans and the Sangre de Cristos, receive more of these storms than do northern areas. Frequently, however, these air masses, often called "summer monsoons," are able to penetrate farther north, reaching northern Colorado and Rocky Mountain National Park, bringing the afternoon thundershowers that send climbers and above-timberline hikers scurrying for cover.

Even though summers are very sunny, at least 80 percent of summer days receive some cloud cover due to convective storms. A typical summer day starts out cloudless, but as the nearby plains heat up, moist air rises and flows up along the mountain front. In response to colder temperatures encountered as it rises, the air begins to cool, and the water vapor forms clouds. By late afternoon, the clouds reach the saturation point, and rain falls from the sky. By evening, cooling temperatures allow the clouds to dissipate, and the skies become clear and star filled.

Autumn is a time of transition, with more precipitation than in early winter, but less than at the height of the summer. The winter storm patterns haven't yet developed, and the moist, tropical air masses from the

Rainbow over Beaver Meadows.

Gulf of Mexico are retreating southward. For many, September and October are the absolute best time to visit the park. Autumn is characterized by pleasant, bright, sunny days and cool nights, with few thunderstorms. More than 50 percent of the days are clear, and cloud cover occurs only about 20 percent of the time.

The driest time of year is early winter. An average of a half inch of precipitation falls during the months of November, December, January, and

February. As anyone who lives near Estes Park can tell you, early winter isn't really all that good for skiing. In fact, the average January snow depth at Bear Lake, elevation 9,400 feet, is usually only two feet. The snowpack in most years doesn't really get deep until later in the winter.

Precipitation begins to pick up in the spring months. In an average year, more than an inch of precipitation falls during March, April, May, and June. March and April are the snowiest months of the year. By May, more of the precipitation is falling as rain, at least at lower elevations, and Estes Park typically receives two inches of precipitation during this month.

The wettest months are the rainy summer monsoon months of July and August. This precipitation, however, tends to come as intense thunderstorms that last for a few hours rather than as the daylong drizzles that are more common in the spring months.

Temperature and Altitude

As anyone who lives in the plains cities of Loveland, Fort Collins, or Denver knows, when you climb up into the mountains, the temperatures drop with increasing altitude. When the thermometer in Fort Collins registers 90 degrees F, it may be only 60 degrees at 12,000 feet on Trail Ridge Road. This has to do with the density of air at different elevations. At higher elevations, for any given volume of air, molecules are spaced farther apart, so there are fewer molecules to hold heat—and provide oxygen to your lungs, which is why you breathe harder at high elevations (there is one-third less oxygen at 10,000 feet than at sea level). Such differences in temperature are due to decreasing air pressure and density as elevation increases. This allows for expansion of the air, with a resultant loss of heat. A standard rule, all things being equal, is that for every 1,000 feet in elevation gained, there is a corresponding 3.5-degree decrease in temperature. This is known as the lapse rate.

The atmospheric density also affects the moisture-holding ability of air masses. At higher elevations, as air density is decreased, its ability to hold moisture is also decreased. This drying out of the air is exacerbated by the general cooling of air that occurs at higher elevations as well. Cool air holds less moisture than warm air. Both factors contribute to the increasing dryness encountered at higher elevations. In fact, there is typically less snowfall at the highest parts of the Front Range, and the zone of greatest snowfall lies between 9,000 and 11,000 feet. At higher elevations, the cold air and low air density tend to produce fewer snow particles.

The reduced ability of the atmosphere to hold moisture also contributes to steep gradients in temperature between shade and sunny areas at higher elevations, as any hiker can attest. When a cloud passes by, the temperature drops sharply. This same lack of heat-holding also accounts for the large diurnal temperature changes experienced in the mountains. Because the clear mountain air has significantly less ability to hold heat, temperatures drop dramatically when the sun sets.

Another effect of the lower density of molecules found at higher elevations is the greater intensity of the blue color of the sky. With fewer molecules to scatter light, particularly at the shorter wave lengths, which include blue end of the spectrum, the intensity of blue light is increased. The sky really is bluer!

Orographic Lift

When air masses encounter steep mountains, they are forced to rise upward, and as they ascend the slope, the air is cooled by evaporation. Cooling reduces the air mass's ability to hold moisture, and the result is precipitation. This is one reason why there is always more cumulative annual precipitation in the mountains than in the valleys. Faster-moving air masses—as are the rule during winter storms—are forced to rise more rapidly, and as a consequence, they cool more quickly, dropping greater amounts of precipitation. In the Rockies, most of this falls as snow.

As the air mass crosses the mountain barrier and begins its descent down the lee side of the mountains, the air masses are compressed, often accelerate, and are warmed. The average temperature increase is 5.5 degrees per 1,000-foot drop in elevation. Thus, air that may have a temperature of 20 degrees at 12,000 feet on Trail Ridge Road may warm to 42 degrees by the time it reaches Estes Park at 7,800 feet. This process is known as adiabatic heating. This warming effect of descending air is one reason why Estes Park has such an equable winter climate. Despite its high elevation, it's really not that cold a place to live.

As a result of this heating process and the ability of the air to hold more moisture, precipitation stops and clouds evaporate. The descending warm air mass begins to "soak up" moisture (warm air can hold more moisture than cool air). This gives rise to the renowned chinook winds. The relative humidity during a typical chinook may be no more than 10 percent. Chinook means "snow eater" in a Pacific Northwest Indian language, and indeed, during a chinook, snow appears to vanish without even leaving pools of water or puddles. The air just causes the moisture to dissipate.

Thunderheads build over the Colorado River Valley.

Though the wind may be howling during a chinook, the air temperature in sheltered places can be quite warm. Get behind some rocks or trees when a chinook is blowing, and the sunny winter days can be quite pleasant. Chinooks are critical to the survival of elk, bighorn sheep, and other wildlife, since they reduce the overall energy requirements by removing snow cover, making it easier to move about and making forage more easily accessible. The warm average temperatures also reduce the thermal differential between warm-bodied animals and the air.

During the summer, a similar process leads to convective summer storms. Daytime heating of the ground causes the air above it to warm and rise. Warm air can hold more moisture, so the rising air temperature actually permits the air to pull moisture from the ground and the surrounding atmosphere. These moist, warm air masses rise upward as thermals. If the air rises high enough, cooling results and clouds begin to form. The level at which cooling is sufficient to turn water vapor into water droplets is visible as the flat base of the resulting cumulus clouds. Under the right conditions, these cumulus clouds spawn towering thunderheads. The resultant storms produce afternoon showers, lightning, and hail over mountain uplands.

Upslope and Downslope Winds

A slight downslope breeze often develops in the mountains at night, and there is often an upslope breeze during the day. These alternating airflows are the result of differential heating of air. At night, once the sun has set, the clear mountain sky radiates heat back into space and cools rapidly. Since cool air is dense, it begins to slide downhill in response to gravity. This cool airflow displaces warmer air, which tends to flow up the sides of the valleys.

If you've ever taken a walk from a creek bottom upslope in the evening, you may have noticed a significant temperature difference. Since cold air sinks to the lowest point, you'll have a cold night's sleep if you camp in open meadows in the bottom of a valley, unless you have a very warm sleeping bag. Sometimes merely moving upslope a few hundred feet results in a temperature difference of as much as 20 degrees. Often the difference in temperature between midslope and the bottom of a basin can be even more dramatic. One study in Austria found a temperature gradient of 45 degrees between the bottom of the valley and a slope 500 feet above it.

Not surprisingly, this cool air drainage affects plant distribution. Meadows often persist in subalpine basins surrounded by trees due to cool air drainage. Many tree species—particularly the seedlings—are very frost sensitive and simply can't invade areas dominated by cold air pockets. These places remain meadows, while trees cloak the surrounding slopes and high points.

The opposite airflow occurs during the day. As the ground heats up, warm air rises and begins to move upward. Unlike the cold air drainage, however, it doesn't hug the ground. Nevertheless, the upslope winds are obvious and tend to feel warmer than the surrounding air.

Lightning

Lightning is a common phenomenon in the mountains in summer. The risk of being hit by lightning is relatively low. Nevertheless, hikers and climbers traveling on ridges, peaks, and other high places during electric storms are most at risk.

In summer, due to gradual heating of the ground, the air above it begins to warm and rise as a thermal. Eventually, a point is reached where the air cools sufficiently that water vapor turns into water droplets, and cumulus clouds develop. As the moist air continues to rise, thunderheads develop. When the air reaches the freezing point, it forms ice particles, which increase the rate of precipitation. Rain begins to fall from the sky, producing a downward draft, often felt as wind that precedes the rain.

The upward rush of ice and rain particles produces lightning. These carry an electric charge with them as they rise, creating a positive charge in the top of the thunderhead. The bottom of the cloud remains negative. The ground is also positive. Eventually, the buildup of negative charge finds a release in the ground, releasing this energy as a lightning strike. There are also strikes within the clouds, as the imbalances between positive and negative ends of a cloud attempt to equalize.

The rapid heating of air by the lightning bolt creates thunder. The air expands, then compresses suddenly, creating the loud noise. This sound travels about one mile in five seconds. One can calculate how far away a lightning bolt struck by counting the time between the flash and the sound.

To avoid being struck by lightning, stay off ridges and peaks. Even getting slightly on the side of a mountain will significantly reduce your exposure. Stay away from large, single trees. If you can find a clump of small trees in a forest, use that for shelter. Avoid huddling together; that way, if a strike hits nearby, not everyone is likely to be hit.

A tree split by a lightning strike.

The Big Thompson Flood

On July 31, 1976, a huge flood crashed down the Big Thompson River Canyon, killing 139 people (6 others were never found) and washing away 418 homes, dozens of businesses, and vehicles. The flood was the result of unusual weather conditions.

Big Thompson River Canyon, Roosevelt National Forest, site of the 1976 Big Thompson flood.

Nothing in the afternoon buildup of clouds over the Front Range gave any hint that a disaster was about to happen. By 6 p.m., the normal buildup of afternoon thunderheads had occurred. But unlike most summer mountain storms, which are pushed eastward over the plains by high-elevation winds, the growing thunderheads stalled over the headwaters of the Big Thompson drainage. The thunderheads continued to rise, condensing water vapor as they did so. By 7 p.m., water was pouring from the sky. An estimated 10 to 12 inches of rain fell in a few hours. At Drake, halfway down the canyon, the river gauge indicated a flow of 137 cubic feet per second at around 6 p.m., but by 9 p.m., the river was raging past the same spot carrying 31,200 cubic feet per second. Water backed up at the Narrows of the Big Thompson River and rose to a depth of more than nineteen feet. Most of the people who died were killed in their cars trying to outrun the floodwaters. Those who chose instead to climb up the mountainside to higher ground survived. As you can see if you drive up the canyon, people have rebuilt homes and businesses in the same narrow canyon floodplain, setting up another recipe for disaster.

WEATHER CHART

Estes Park, on Eastern Slope of Continental Divide, elevation 7,500 feet

Month	Average High Temperatures	Average Low Temperatures	Average Precipitation
Jan.	38	17	0.42
Feb.	41	18	0.39
Mar.	44	20	0.78
Apr.	53	26	1.34
May	62	34	2.13
June	73	41	1.64
July	79	46	2.13
Aug.	76	44	1.97
Sept.	70	37	1.21
Oct.	60	30	0.76
Nov.	47	22	0.54
Dec.	40	18	0.52

Record High: 90
Record Low: –39

Granby, on Western Slope of Continental Divide, elevation 8,210 feet

Month	Average High Temperatures	Average Low Temperatures	Average Precipitation
Jan.	28	01	1.17
Feb.	31	01	0.82
Mar.	37	09	1.20
Apr.	47	20	1.07
May	59	29	1.34
June	69	36	1.20
July	75	41	1.51
Aug.	73	40	1.73
Sept.	68	33	1.11
Oct.	56	24	0.75
Nov.	40	14	0.88
Dec.	30	05	1.43

Record High: 88
Record Low: –41

GEOLOGY

Rocky Mountain National Park owes much of its scenic beauty to its geological history. The uplift of mountains, the eruption of volcanoes, the sculpting by glaciers, and the annual occurrence of floods, rockslides, freezing, and thawing have all shaped the landscape. These kinds of geological events are recorded in the rocks, and this record spans nearly 1.8 billion years! Yet few rocks that old remain in the park; most were eroded away.

The most obvious physical features of the park are its mountains and peaks. The park straddles the Continental Divide and is one of the highest parts of the 180-mile-long Front Range (the Mummy Range in Rocky Mountain National Park is a subset of the Front Range). The Front Range stretches from the Arkansas River on the south, north to Wyoming, where it splits into the Medicine Bow Range and Laramie Range. It is about 40 miles wide and is bordered on the east by the Denver Basin and on the west by several large valleys, including North Park, Middle Park, and South Park.

The rocks making up its core are among the oldest exposed anywhere in the western United States. They consist of metamorphic gneiss and schists approximately 1.7 billion years old, plus granitic rocks of a slightly younger age.

The other major range in the park is the Never Summer Range. Its geological history and origins are quite different from that of the Front Range. The rocks making up the Never Summer Range are much younger than those found in the Front Range and originated from volcanic activity some 29 to 25 million years ago.

In the broadest terms, the Front Range was uplifted beginning 70 million years ago, and the subsequent erosion of overlying sedimentary rocks exposed the crystalline core of the range. This was partially covered with

The oldest rocks in Rocky Mountain National Park are schists and gneisses more than 1.7 billion years old, with younger intrusions of granite.

volcanic debris from the Never Summer Range. Further erosion exposed metamorphic rocks as well as the granitic cores in both mountain uplifts. These were then glaciated to create its current form.

Understanding the landscape we see today requires going back in geological time to discover the forces that gave rise to the present-day geological setting.

Origins of Rocks

All rocks on earth can be classified as one of three major rock types, sedimentary, igneous, or metamorphic, depending upon their origins and geological history. Sedimentary rocks were made from sediments like sand and mud or organic matter (such as the ferns and other vegetation that created the coal beds found in the United States) typically lain down in oceans or lakes. Igneous rocks are those "born of fire"—for example, from the lava from a volcano. Metamorphic rock is derived from either igneous or sedimentary rock, or even from preexisting metamorphic rock. Such rocks are recrystallized by heat and pressure into something else. For example, marble is metamorphosed limestone.

The most common sedimentary rocks found in the West are sandstone, shale, limestone, and siltstone. These kinds of sedimentary rocks are spectacularly displayed in the red rock country of the Colorado Plateau in western Colorado and southern Utah. Sedimentary rocks are common on the flanks of the Front Range outside of Rocky Mountain National Park, but they are virtually nonexistent in the park. Most of the rocks exposed in Rocky Mountain National Park are of igneous or metamorphic origins.

The most abundant metamorphic rocks in the park are gneiss (pronounced "nice") and schist. Gneiss and schist are formed from sedimentary or, in some cases, igneous rocks that have been changed by heat and pressure.

Gneiss is derived from sedimentary rocks with a high sand content, such as sandstone. Most gneiss has telltale signs of its former sedimentary origin, seen as swirled or slightly wavy horizontal lines, something like the marbled look of partially stirred cake batter. This kind of swirled, marbled gneiss is fairly common in Rocky Mountain National Park. Sedimentary rocks that have a lot of clays in them prior to metamorphism become schists. Schists have an abundance of mica, and the flat, shiny flakes are easily split along the mica layers. Schists are also found in the park and tend to be darker than the gneiss, usually a gray-black, with the shiny flakes of mica easily observed.

Most other rocks exposed in the park are igneous. There are two kinds of igneous rock: intrusive (plutonic) and extrusive (volcanic). Plutonic igneous rocks are formed when molten rock cools deep in the earth. They tend to have large crystals. If the magma reaches the surface to explode or flow from a volcano, it cools rapidly and displays almost no crystalliza-

Banded layering in gneiss belies its sedimentary origins.

tion. For example, the Lava Cliffs seen on the Trail Ridge Road consist of welded tuff or hot volcanic ash ejected during an explosion and subsequently fused together as rock.

The most abundant igneous rock exposed in Rocky Mountain National Park is granite. There were two major episodes of granitic emplacement. The majority of granites in the park developed as small plutons or blobs of molten rock that rose through fractures and faults into the preexisting metamorphic gneiss and schist some 1.4 billion years ago. A more recent emplacement of granitic plutons occurred in the Never Summer Range approximately 29 to 25 million years ago, and this granite is now exposed in some of the higher peaks in that range. Because these granites cooled slowly at great depth, large, coarse-grained crystals formed in the rock matrix. One way to identify these granitic rocks is the presence of these salt-and-pepper-colored grains in a light gray or slightly pink matrix.

The gneiss, schist, and granite found in Rocky Mountain National Park are very old rocks. They were part of the crystalline rock core of the North American continent known as Precambrian basement rocks. At the time that these ancient rocks were formed, none of the continents, including North America, had their current shape or position.

Since granite is never formed on the surface of the earth, visible granite is the result of uplifting and the erosion of overlying rocks. Most of the higher, rugged mountain ranges in the West, including the Tetons, Wind River Range, Sawtooth Mountains, and Sierra Nevada, are composed primarily of granites. The most common granite exposed in the park is known as Silver Plume Granite. Outcrops of the slightly pinkish Silver Plume Granite occur in the central portion of the Front Range. In the park, they are most common east of the Continental Divide and in the west near Shadow Mountain Lake and Grand Lake. Longs Peak, the highest point in Rocky Mountain National Park, is composed of Silver Plume Granite, as is the section of Trail Ridge Road between Rainbow Curve and the Road Cut. Ancient granite also makes up McGregor Mountain, Deer Mountain, Hagues Peak, Lumpy Ridge, and Bighorn Mountain, as well as others of the higher mountains in the park.

Because of their different origins and relative hardness, erosion of each rock type produces distinctive formations. Granite gives rise to rounded mountains, such as McGregor Mountain and Lumpy Ridge; gneiss and schist are more easily fractured into jagged peaks, such as the Sharkstooth and Hayden Spire. The differential erosion of both rock types is visible

A tor along the Tundra World Nature Trail. The top part of the formation consists of schist, a metamorphic rock formed from clay, while the lighter bottom part of the formation is granite, an intrusive igneous rock formed deep in the earth.

along the alpine Tundra World Nature Trail, where you can see tors created by caprock of dark schist on top of lighter granite.

Geological History

Plate tectonics provides a unifying theory and a contextual framework for understanding how the mountains we see in Rocky Mountain National Park came into existence. Plate tectonics can be thought of as shaping the foundation and walls of a house, while more recent events like ice-age glaciation put the finishing touches upon the landscape, something like decorating an individual room.

According to plate theory, the earth's crust is made up of several dozen plates. North America is one plate, and the Pacific Ocean basin is another. These plates float on the earth's mantle like icebergs in a river. Deep convention currents in the earth's mantle drag these plates about the earth's surface at a rate of about an inch per year, causing some plates to collide, others to break up, and some to move past each other.

Each plate consists of a relatively stable core known as a craton, typically composed of crystalline gneiss, schist, and granites. The Canadian Shield of the northern United States and much of central Canada makes up the old core of the North American continent. The edge of this stable craton is known as the mobile belt. New additions to the continent, and most of the mountain building, occur along this leading edge of the continent. The western part of North America, where the majority of active mountain building and volcanic activity is occurring, represents the mobile belt of the North American continental plate.

Typically, continental plates are composed of lighter granitic rocks, whereas ocean basins are dominated by heavier iron-rich basalt. When a continental plate meets an ocean plate, the heavier ocean plate dives beneath the continental plate. As it moves deeper into the mantle, it eventually melts. This molten rock then rises toward the surface, burning a hole up through the overlying continental rock. Sometimes it reaches the surface to pour out as a volcanic eruption, or it may cool in place below the surface, often forming granitic plutons or bodies of granite rock. This is happening right now along the Pacific Northwest coast, where the westward-moving North American continent is overriding an ocean basin plate, which is melting, providing the magma for the region's large volcanoes, such as Mount Rainier, Mount St. Helens, Mount Hood, and Mount Shasta.

The pressure of colliding or subducting plates often crumples the plate surface, breaking it up into faults. Pressure from plate movement can then cause rocks to move up or drop along fault lines. This is exactly what created the mountains of Rocky Mountain National Park. The Front Range of Colorado is a fault-defined range that was created by the collision of plates. Along one such fault, Longs Peak has been pushed up more than four miles above similar-age granitic rock buried beneath sediments on the nearby plains.

Longs Peak is a block of granite that has been uplifted more than four miles along faults over similar-age granite lying beneath the Great Plains east of the Front Range.

Though the crystalline core rocks that make up the mountains in the park are very ancient, and resemble in many ways the crystalline core rocks that make up the North America craton, they nevertheless originated elsewhere and only later were added on to the North American continent. These ancient igneous and metamorphic rocks were once part

Outcrop of 1.4-billion-year-old Silver Plume Granite on Deer Mountain.

of a large island or minicontinent, something like today's New Zealand. Millions of years ago, long before the present-day mountains rose, the ancient North American continent overrode the ocean basin upon which this island was perched. The island mass, sometimes called the Colorado Arc Terrane, was more than 700 miles wide. It collided with the old edge of the North American continent, known as the Wyoming craton. Rather than diving beneath it, as occurs with the basalts that make up the ocean basins, the lighter granite, gneiss, and schist rocks of the Colorado Arc Terrane island minicontinent were welded onto the growing southern margin of the Wyoming craton. Today a large belt of rock, known as the Cheyenne Suture Zone, runs across southern Wyoming and marks the boundary between these two geological provinces.

The addition of this large island minicontinent to the edge of the continent led to igneous rock formation. Most likely, a series of volcanoes were created as the ocean basin continued its slide under the North American continent, providing the magma source for granitic intrusions that occurred 1.4 billion years ago. These granitic plutons (molten magma) were intruded into the gneiss and schists, with each major pulse creating a distinct granite, including what is now known as the Silver Plume Granite.

After the addition of this, a long period of erosion ensued, which wore the region down to a featureless plain and removed all rock records of that time period.

By the Cambrian Period, which began 570 million years ago, the emergent North American plate was located in tropical latitudes. As a result of ongoing tectonic forces, oceans covered most of the land now occupied by the Rockies and then retreated from the region. This happened countless times. There was an explosion of life during this period, with the evolution of numerous species of shellfish, worms, and jellyfish.

By the early Devonian Period, which began 410 million years ago, North America was joined with Europe and Asia to form a much larger continent geologists call Laurasia. Seas still advanced and retreated up until the Pennsylvanian Period, some 300 million years ago. During this long period of time, life-forms evolved from simple shellfish into fishes and amphibians.

Then, approximately 300 million years ago, when early forms of reptiles were spreading across the globe, continental collisions led to the uplifting of the area that is now part of Rocky Mountain National Park. It is believed that a huge plate consisting of South America and Africa collided with Laurasia, and the shock waves from this collision intensely deformed and wrenched the southwest portion of the North American plate that now includes Colorado. Modest highlands of approximately 2,000 feet rose to form the Ancestral Front Range Highland. The Ouachita Mountains in Arkansas are thought to be remnants of these ancient mountains. These highlands were then attacked by erosive forces, including downcutting from streams, which carried away the overlying layer of younger rocks to expose the core basement rocks again. These basement rocks were eroded to a flat plain.

By 290 million years ago, all the continents were joined together (with the exception of China) to create a supercontinent known as Pangaea. This changing configuration of landmass, with a giant continent and a reduced ocean margin, affected climatic conditions. A huge interior area far from any ocean resulted in desertlike conditions. This change in climatic conditions, combined with the loss of shallow ocean basins, resulted in a huge extinction of species, particularly marine organisms. On land, great numbers of amphibian and reptile species also became extinct. This mass extinction soon paved the way for greater development of reptile species that were less dependent upon water. Reptiles soon came to dominate the arid lands of Pangaea, eventually giving rise to the reign of dinosaurs.

Sometime around 205 million years ago, Pangaea began to break apart, with North America starting to peel away from Europe. As this movement continued, the Atlantic Ocean opened up in its wake. By the Cretaceous Period, from 135 to 65 million years ago, dinosaurs dominated the globe. Early in the Cretaceous Period, approximately 130 million years ago, an inland sea split North America, covering the future Rockies with sediments up to 8,000 feet in thickness. Some of these sediments, known as the Dakota sandstone, can be seen today along the flank of the Front Range along U.S. Route 34 between Loveland and Estes Park.

By the late Cretaceous Period, North America began to override the Farallon Plate, part of the Pacific Ocean basin. The force of this collision created severe compression and faulting along the western edge of the continent. By 70 million years ago, just before the extinction of dinosaurs, the westward movement of the continental core had accelerated, and the effects of this continuing compression reached the interior of the continent and began to push up the Rocky Mountains in what is known as the Laramide Orogeny (mountain building). The Laramide Orogeny is responsible for the uplift of the entire Rocky Mountain Cordillera, from Alaska to Mexico.

The uplift also further fractured the crust, allowing mineralized solutions to rise along faults in a fifty-mile-wide belt from the San Juan Mountains near Durango to the Front Range near Golden. These mineralized solutions eventually cooled, creating the rich mineralized ore veins containing gold, copper, and silver that supported Colorado's mining industry.

Most of Rocky Mountain National Park lies outside of this mineralized belt, and the lack of significant mineralization is likely one reason conservationists were able to get the area set aside as a national park. Had it been within the mineralized belt, mining interests likely would have prevented its designation.

The Laramide mountain building uplifted the Front Range, as well as the Medicine Bow, Park, and Gore Ranges, all of which were once part of the old Ancestral Front Range Highland. North and Middle Parks were both part of structural sag in the old Ancestral Front Range Highland that remained as valleys during this period of mountain uplift.

As the Front Range rose, some of the overlying layers of sedimentary rocks were eroded away, while other layers slid off the rising mountain core and were stacked on end near the edge of the mountains, where they rise out of the plains. The Flat Irons by Boulder are one example of these uptilted old sedimentary rocks. You can see some of these overlying stacked sedimentary rock as you approach Rocky Mountain National Park on U.S. Route 34 along the Big Thompson River. The first rock formations you encounter as you wind along the river are uptilted layers of shale and sandstone. After crossing these "foothills," you enter a narrower canyon of much harder rock that makes up the old crystalline core of the continent.

The Tertiary Period began 65 million years ago, around the time of the extinction of the dinosaurs, and ended just 2 million years ago, when the Pleistocene Period began. By the middle part of the Tertiary, uplift had slowed, and erosional forces once again wore down the mountains to almost a flat surface. The nearly level surfaces of Longs Peak, Terra Tomah Mountain, Deer Mountain, and Flattop Mountain reflect this flat preglacial topography.

Flat Irons by Boulder are uplifted sedimentary rocks that once capped the rocks now exposed in the Front Range high peaks. As these peaks were pushed upward, the overlying sedimentary layers slid eastward to rest against the flank of the rising mountain range.

Specimen Mountain, near the headwaters of the Cache la Poudre River, consists of volcanic ash and welded tuff erupted from volcanoes in the Never Summer Range some 38 million years ago.

A third period of uplift followed, beginning some 38 million years ago, about the time when birds and mammals were diversifying across the globe. The Never Summer Range was pushed up at this time. Between 29 and 25 million years ago, a series of volcanoes not unlike today's Cascade Range in Washington and Oregon erupted from Never Summer Range peaks such as Mount Richtofen, blanketing much of the ancient crystalline core basement rocks with a layer of lava, welded tuff, and ash. Subsequent erosion associated with later uplift of the Front Range stripped away most of these more recent volcanic rocks, leaving only a few remaining outcrops, such as Lava Cliffs on the Trail Ridge Road and Specimen Mountain near the headwaters of the Cache la Poudre River.

Some of the magma feeding the Never Summer Range volcanoes failed to reach the surface, cooling in place deep in the earth. As the range was uplifted higher, the overlying sedimentary and volcanic rocks were removed, exposing the magma chambers of these volcanoes. Today you can see these Tertiary-age granitic rocks exposed in Mount Nimbus, Mount Cumulus, and other peaks of the Never Summer Range.

Though separated by less than ten miles, the granites in the Never Summer Range are more than 1.6 billion years younger than the granites that make up the Front Range, reflecting their very different origins. A large fault separates the Never Summer Range from the Front Range. Here, through the shattered rock that marks this fractured part of the earth, the Colorado River has carved its valley.

The last period of uplift occurred in the late Pliocene Epoch. At approximately 5 million years ago, about the time when the earliest humans were first beginning to evolve on the African savanna, the Front Range reached its present height.

Glaciation

The finishing touches on Rocky Mountain National Park's peaks occurred during the Quaternary Period, which includes both the Pleistocene ice ages and the last 10,000 years, known as the Holocene Epoch. Approximately 2 million years ago, there was a shift in the climate to cooler and moister conditions. The greater moisture coupled with cooler temperatures led to copious snowfall and less summertime melting. As snows accumulated in the alpine basins and valleys, glaciers formed in the higher areas of the Front Range and eventually began to move downslope in response to gravity.

The last ice age was not a continuous period of cold and snow. There were several major periods of glaciation, followed by warmer interludes when the ice melted completely away. In Rocky Mountain National Park, there is evidence for three major glacial advances, although only the two most recent are easily observed by visitors.

The oldest, known as the Pre-Bull Lake Glaciation, occurred between 738,000 and 302,000 years ago. There were likely multiple advances and retreats during this time, although the evidence is scanty. Only two parts of the park have been identified as Pre-Bull Lake glacial deposits. One is by the Aspenglen campground, and the other is near where State Route 7 crosses the North Fork St. Vrain River in Wild Basin.

The oldest glacial deposits readily seen in the park are from the Bull Lake Glaciation, named for a lake on the eastern slope of the Wind River Range in Wyoming. There were at least two, and perhaps more, advances and retreats of Bull Lake glaciers, which began some 300,000 years ago and ended approximately 130,000 years ago. Much of the evidence for the Bull Lake Glaciation was overrun and destroyed by the last glacial advance, known as the Pinedale Glaciation, and most of the glacial debris found in the park today is from the Pinedale glacial advance.

The Pinedale Glaciation is named for glacial moraines and other debris from the Wind River Range near Pinedale, Wyoming, where geologists first studied this glacial advance. The Pinedale Glaciation occurred in the Front Range between 30,000 and 13,750 years ago and reached its maximum extent approximately 23,000 to 21,000 years ago. At this time, glacial ice cloaked most of the higher basins and filled the valleys.

The west slope of the Front Range received more moisture than the east slope. West-slope Pinedale-era glaciers were typically longer, with the largest being the twenty-mile-long Colorado River Glacier, whose terminal moraine can be seen as a series of low islands in the south end of Shadow Mountain Reservoir. East-slope glaciers were shorter, with most no more than nine to ten miles in length, although the glacier that filled Forest Canyon was thirteen miles long at its maximum extent. A warming trend eliminated most of the glaciers by 12,000 years ago.

The rugged bowls and cliffs of the Gorge Lakes area were created by ice-age glaciers.

Taylor Glacier, above Loch Vale, was formed during the Little Ice Age, a cooling trend that began in 1400 A.D. and ended around 1850.

Since the end of the Pleistocene, four minor glacial advances have been recorded in the Front Range. Unlike the major ice-age glaciers, which filled entire valleys, the Holocene glaciers are very small, most covering less than a mile in area. The existing small glaciers found today in Rocky Mountain National Park, such as the Tyndall, Taylor, and Andrews Glaciers, were all formed during the Little Ice Age, a cooling trend that began in the 1400s and ended in the 1850s. Given the arid climate of the Front

Range, it's surprising that any glaciers exist at all. These tiny glaciers survive because they are situated in north- or northeast-facing cirques, where they are shaded from the sun. In addition, they are replenished by wind-blown snow, which adds significantly to the annual accumulations.

Glacial Features

The physical appearance of Rocky Mountain National Park was greatly shaped and influenced by glaciation. Glaciers work primarily through abrasion and grinding combined with plucking. When snow reaches a depth of 100 to 200 feet or so, the weight causes it to crystallize into ice, and it begins to flow downhill. The movement of glaciers is unusual. While the surface of the ice remains brittle, the great accumulation of snow and ice that makes up a glacier is so heavy that, as a result of great pressure, the bottom of the ice deforms and becomes somewhat plastic, almost liquid. The bottom of the glacier almost oozes downhill like thick, cold toothpaste. As this ice flows over obstacles such as knobs and ridges in the bedrock, pressure is increased upon the ice, leading to greater plastic flow. Once this particular segment of the glacier is over the high point, pressure is relieved, and the ice becomes more brittle and refreezes.

During this continual flow-and-freeze process, the glacier plucks loose rock from the bedrock and freezes it in the bottom and sides of the glacier. Through this process of freeze, thaw, and refreeze, with the plucking and grinding away of rock, the continually moving ice gradually creates a number of distinctive glacial features, such as cirques, horns, tarns, and arêtes.

Perhaps the easiest to recognize are the bowl-shaped amphitheaters that look as if a giant ice cream scoop carved them. These glacier-carved basins are known by the French word *cirque*. One excellent example of a cirque is visible from the Forest Canyon overlook on Terra Tomah Mountain, and another is the bowl-like basin at the head of the Fall River by the Alpine Visitor Center.

Sometimes these basins fill with water, creating cirque lakes. One of the most famous cirque lakes is Chasm Lake, below Longs Peak. Other cirque lakes in the park include Fern, Lawn, Odessa, Blue, and Shelf Lakes.

Glaciers typically flow down existing water-carved valleys. As they do so, they steepen the valley sides and flatten the bottom; the end result is a characteristic U-shaped valley. The differences between a narrow, water-carved, V-shaped valley, like the lower Big Thompson River valley outside

A large valley glacier once flowed down the Fall River Valley, carving it into its present U shape.

the park, and a U-shaped valley, like Forest Canyon, are fairly easy to discern. Other glacier-carved valleys in the park include the upper Fall River, Upper North St. Vrain Valley, Cache la Poudre Valley, and Kawuneeche Valley in the upper Colorado River Valley.

At times, so much ice accumulates in the higher headwaters of a glacier that pressure forces the ice to flow upslope as it oozes over passes and low divides. This is exactly what happened when the massive glacier that once filled the Upper Colorado Valley flowed over Milner Pass. Sheep Rock, near Poudre Lake along the Trail Ridge Road, was beveled smooth by ice flowing upslope from the Colorado River Valley to the west. A tongue of the giant Colorado River Glacier pushed across Milner Pass and flowed down the Upper Cache la Poudre drainage.

Since smaller drainages collect smaller amounts of snow, tributary glaciers typically don't carve as deep a valley as the larger glaciers occupying the main valleys. As a result, when glaciers retreat, these side valleys are typically left hanging above the main valley. Such side valleys are known as hanging valleys and are often marked by waterfalls. Numerous hanging valleys occupy cirques in the Never Summer Range above the Upper

Colorado River Valley. Chiquita Creek, Fern Creek, and Roaring River all occupy hanging valleys in the Front Range.

Glacial moraines are another of the more obvious features seen in Rocky Mountain National Park. As a glacier flows down a valley, it pushes loose rock and other debris in front of it, much as a bulldozer might shove dirt in front of its blade. Glaciers also rip rock loose from the surrounding valley walls and carry this material along, embedded in their ice. When a glacier melts, it leaves all this debris piled up in low hills or mounds that mimic the shape of the glacier. Those moraines on the side of a glacier are known as lateral moraines, and the U-shaped moraines that mark the greatest advance of the ice are called terminal moraines. Moraines are easily recognized by the random, unsorted collections of rock debris, boulders, and soil all mixed together.

Obvious moraines are found north of Longs Peak and are easily seen from Moraine Park and the Longs Peak overview on the Trail Ridge Road. The low hills on either side of Moraine Park were deposited by the Big

East Inlet glacial moraine. Glacial moraine can be identified by the unsorted mix of large boulders, small rocks, and sand.

Bear Lake was formed when a large chunk of ice left stranded in glacial moraine melted to create a small kettle lake.

Thompson Glacier and are lateral moraines. Another lateral moraine lies along the slope of Bighorn Mountain in the Fall River Valley. A third obvious moraine is cut by the road to the East Intake Trailhead by Grand Lake. Indeed, Grand Lake village is built upon the same moraine. On the drive up to the Bear Lake parking lot, the road crosses the edge of the Bierstadt Moraine.

Wild Basin is one of the few areas of the park where you can see moraines from all three known park glaciations: the Pre-Bull, Bull, and Pinedale glacial advances. Where State Route 7 crosses the North St. Vrain River drainage by Wild Basin, terminal moraine and lateral moraines mark the farthest advance of the Wild Basin Glacier.

Sometimes water is backed up behind a moraine to create a lake. Grand Lake was formed behind a terminal moraine. Other moraine-dammed lakes once existed in Moraine Valley and Horseshoe Park. Sediments subsequently filled these lakes. The flat valleys in these parks are today large meadows.

Small lakes, often without an obvious inlet or outlet, are created when chunks of ice trapped in the moraine melts. These are known as kettle lakes. Kettle lakes include Bear, Copeland, Sheep, and Dream Lakes.

Erratics and striations are other evidence of the former existence of glaciers. Erratics are boulders that have been transported some distance by glaciers, then dropped, so they are now out of place. When a glacier flows over bedrock, rock and sand embedded in the base of the ice gouges scratches, known as striations, into the bedrock.

Ongoing Geological Events

Floods, avalanches, landslides, and freeze-thaw events all continue to rework and change the face of Rocky Mountain National Park. One of the popular entries into Rocky Mountain National Park is the drive from Loveland along Highway 34, following the Big Thompson River Canyon, scene of the massive 1976 flood.

Another recent geological event occurred when a dam on Lawn Lake in the Mummy Range failed, sending 18,000 cubic feet per second of muddy water cascading down the Roaring River Valley. When the flood

Debris from the Lawn Lake floods. An irrigation dam on the lake failed, sending 18,000 cubic feet per second of water careening down the Roaring River Valley.

Stone rings on Mount Chapin in the Mummy Range. Frost heaving creates the rings.

reached the flat floor of Horseshoe Park, it spread out, dumping most of its load of boulders, sand, and mud in a giant alluvial fan at the mouth of the canyon. The fan now covers forty-two acres with debris. Some of the boulders carried by the floodwater weighed as much as 450 tons.

Another interesting geological phenomenon found in the alpine areas of the park is patterned ground. This results from the freezing and thawing of alpine soils, which pushes small rocks to the surface, creating polygon formations, stripes, and other symmetrical designs.

Rocky Mountain National Park owes much of its scenic quality to its geological history. Knowledge of this history will greatly increase your enjoyment of a visit to the park.

HISTORY

Early Humans

The earliest humans to roam Colorado, and perhaps Rocky Mountain National Park, were the Paleo-Indians (*Paleo* is Greek for ancient). The Paleo-Indians entered what is now Colorado about 12,000 years ago, at the tail end of the last major ice age, when small glaciers still filled some of the alpine valleys. The climate was cooler and wetter than today. The Paleo-Indians were primarily big-game hunters and pursued several big-game species that are now extinct, such as woolly mammoths, giant bison, and huge bears, as well as many of the species still living in Colorado today, including elk, antelope, and deer.

These early hunters did not have bows and arrows; these were not invented until much later. Their prime hunting weapon was the spear. The early stone spear points were distinctive in shape and size. The people who crafted them were known as the Clovis people, after Clovis, New Mexico, where the first examples were discovered. Clovis hunters concentrated on killing large mammals, such as woolly mammoths. They had to get very close to the animals to throw a spear hard enough to penetrate the thick hide. Undoubtedly, killing a mammoth was difficult and fraught with danger.

The Clovis culture lasted about 1,000 years. The climate continued to become warmer and drier, and many of the ice-age mammals became extinct during this period. Many archaeologists blame their extinction on Clovis hunters. Whatever the cause of this mass extinction, humans had to change their hunting methods to concentrate on game smaller than the huge mammoths, such as bison, and they developed a new stone point that was shorter. These points were known as Folsom points, after Folsom, New Mexico, where the first examples of these unique spear points were

Lake Granby in Middle Park. Stone-age hunters often crossed the Front Range to what are today North, Middle, and South Parks to hunt ice-age mammals such as bison.

found. One of the most important Folsom sites in the United States is the Lindenmeier site, located in the foothills of the Rockies near Fort Collins, not more than forty miles from Rocky Mountain National Park. Animal bones found on the site include antelope, bison, rabbit, wolf, fox, and turtle. Hundreds of obsidian scrapers and spear points were also found at the site. Chemical analysis of these points has determined that the source of much of this obsidian was in what is now Yellowstone National Park. This indicates that either these early hunters traveled hundreds of miles in their hunting and gathering excursions, or early trade routes were already established.

Folsom hunters were not confined to valley bottoms but apparently made treks to the mountains to hunt or crossed mountain passes en route to high mountain valleys like Middle and South Parks. Sites as high as 10,000 feet have been discovered, and it's reasonable to assume that some Folsom hunters may have hunted or traveled through what is now Rocky Mountain National Park. At least a few suspected Clovis and Folsom projectile points have been found on the alpine tundra in Rocky Mountain

National Park, evidence that these people likely crossed the mountains while moving from one hunting area to another.

Like the Clovis tradition, the Folsom culture was relatively short-lived as well. By 10,000 years ago, Folsom points were replaced by a new style of spear point from a culture known as the Plano tradition. The Plano tradition lasted 3,000 years. Plano sites are abundant in Colorado and are often associated with bison kills. Plano people would stage organized hunts in which bison were driven into ravines or over cliffs, to be speared to death by waiting hunters. One Colorado Plano archaeological site yielded the bones of at least 300 bison that were killed in such a mass slaughter.

Responding to changing climatic conditions, the Plano culture gave way to the Archaic tradition around 7,000 years ago. The climate at this time turned considerably drier and warmer, and there is evidence that people abandoned the plains and moved into the wetter and cooler mountains, following their major prey. Archaic people may have lived year-round in high mountain valleys like North Park, pursuing large mammals such as elk, antelope, and a smaller kind of bison that evolved from the larger ice-age animals. Archaic people diversified their diet, hunting smaller game and gathering roots, berries, and other foods. Rabbits and other small game now composed a significant portion of the diet. Big game was pursued in winter, when deep snow often trapped elk and deer. Stalking the animals on snowshoes, hunters could often approach close enough to kill them with clubs.

Numerous finds of spear points, scrapers, and other implements on Flattop Mountain, Fall River Canyon, Forest Canyon, Chapin Pass, and elsewhere in the park demonstrate that these ancient people regularly traversed the area that is now Rocky Mountain National Park, although it's doubtful that they lived here.

The Archaic culture gradually gave way to the Woodland culture, whose center was in the Mississippi Valley. The Woodland people developed pottery and farming. These traditions led to more permanent villages and greater human population density. Most of these developments did not immediately affect people living near Rocky Mountain National Park, who no doubt continued a migratory hunting tradition. One technological advance transferred from the Woodland culture to people in Colorado had a significant effect even upon the hunters and gatherers: the bow and arrow, which Colorado tribes acquired between 400 and 650 A.D.

The bow and arrow allowed a hunter to kill an animal at a considerable distance, with less danger to the hunter and a greater chance of surprising the animal. With the bow and arrow now the major hunting weapon, projectile points shrank even further, becoming relatively dainty and fragile.

Game drives became more popular at this time. Along the spine of the mountains, there are numerous game-drive sites, where stone piles funneled frightened animals toward waiting hunters. Bighorn sheep were among the most popular species to hunt. Along the Continental Divide west of Denver, there are more than thirty-five game-drive sites in a fifteen-mile stretch of mountains. Similar sites have been found on the alpine tundra in Rocky Mountain National Park.

The people living along the Front Range of the Rockies developed a seasonal migration pattern. They spent the winter living among the hogbacks along the foothills of the mountains, where game was relatively abundant and winter snows were typically shallow. In the spring, they migrated north toward the present Wyoming border and crossed the Continental Divide to the North Platte River, where they hunted bison, elk, and other big game. They continued southward into Middle Park, and then climbed eastward over the Continental Divide to hunt bighorn sheep and other big game high in the mountains. Once the snow began in the fall, they descended from these high-elevation camps, packs laden with meat, back down to the foothills to spend the winter. This all was done without the aid of horses. All supplies and food were carried on the people's backs or in small packs tied to their dogs.

Historic Indian Tribes

Most of the historic tribes that lived on the Colorado Plains adjacent to the Front Range entered the state in relatively recent times. One of the great cultural changes that gave rise to rapid migration and movement was the acquisition of the horse from the Spanish. By 1640, southern tribes in New Mexico and elsewhere had stolen horses from Spanish settlements in Mexico and New Mexico. By the mid-1700s, the horses had spread throughout the western United States and revolutionized Indian culture, particularly on the plains. They allowed hunters to pursue the migratory herds of bison and other big game, ranging hundreds of miles on hunting expeditions, and providing a more stable source of food. Greater food resources coupled with the mobility of the horse led to the development of a warrior culture, where status in the tribe was garnered by bravery in battle. The horse also upset traditional alliances and territorial boundaries between tribes. Not all tribes acquired the horse at the same time, and mounted warriors were often able to dominate their neighbors until they in turn acquired sufficient horses to offer a counterresistance.

Plains tribes whose territories overlapped what is today Colorado included the Kiowa, Cheyenne, Jicarilla Apaches, Utes, Comanches, and Arapaho. The Utes are a Shoshonean-speaking people, related to the Aztec language groups of Mexico. It is thought that they invaded western Colorado around 1,000 years ago, moving north from Mexico. The Utes were hunters and gatherers, moving with the seasons to exploit different food resources. By the 1680s, the Utes were trading regularly with the Spanish, in particular seeking horses, which they valued so highly that they would sell their children into slavery to obtain a prized mount. The Utes began to forage farther afield, raiding the Apaches on the plains of eastern Colorado and roaming south to plunder the Spanish settlements in New Mexico. They also made regular trips to the plains to hunt bison. Eventually, they met resistance from the plains-dwelling Comanche, who had obtained guns from French fur traders and were not only mounted but also armed. The Comanche drove the aggressive Utes back into the mountains. After this, except for an occasional bison hunt, the Utes confined their movements to the mountains, particularly the large parks and the western slopes of Colorado. It is probable, however, that they occasionally traveled through what is now Rocky Mountain National Park, over traditional pathways like Trail Ridge and other passes across the Continental Divide.

The dominance of the Utes was seriously challenged by the arrival in Colorado of the Arapaho tribe around 1790. The Arapaho are an Algonquian-speaking people who originated in the lake country of Manitoba. Evidence suggests that they had migrated to the northern Great Plains by 1650, where they split into two groups. The Gros Ventre branch of the tribe roamed the area north of the Missouri River in Montana and into Canada, while the Arapaho group moved southward and were in Colorado by the late 1700s.

Like their neighbors, they hunted bison on horseback, lived in tepees, and traveled widely in search of game and plunder. They wintered in sheltered canyons along the Front Range; the Cache la Poudre and Big Thompson River Canyons were favorites. The Arapaho made regular treks into the mountains, following routes like Trail Ridge to hunt game in

Utes and Arapaho were both historically present in what is today Rocky Mountain National Park, often using Trail Ridge to cross the Continental Divide. Many place names in the park, including Kawuneeche Valley, pictured here, are of Native American origin.

the mountain parks, such as North Park west of the Continental Divide. Tepee rings have been found high in the mountains of Rocky Mountain National Park. Oral history suggests that Longs Peak was the site of an eagle trap, although the first whites to climb the mountain found no evidence of any previous human occupation. Many places in the park have Arapaho names, including Haiyaha Lake (meaning "rock"), Haynach Lakes ("snow water"), Kawuneeche Valley ("wolf leader"), Nokoni Lake ("traveling in circle"), and Mount Wuh ("bear").

Although never numerous, probably never exceeding 2,500 people, the Arapaho were aggressive, and almost from their arrival in the South Platte country, they continually waged war on the Utes. At least one white, Charles Strobie, who was living with a band of Utes in North Park, was an eyewitness to a battle between the two old adversaries. In 1865, Strobie accompanied a group of Utes who fought some Arapaho in Middle Park. He reported that the Utes took seven scalps.

Albert Sprague, one of the first white settlers of Estes Park, noted that "Indians made Estes Park a summer resort, as evidence of their summer camps were everywhere throughout the park when the white pioneer came."

By the 1820s, most of these tribes, including the Arapaho, regularly visited trading posts set up by white fur traders along the rivers of the plains. From the traders, they obtained blankets, pots, knives, and food staples. In later years, rifles were also obtained. With rifles and horses, Indian hunting and warfare was revolutionized. Different tribes were continually overpowering their neighbors, overtaking territory. The Utes were driven into the mountains of western Colorado largely by hostile tribes that had recently invaded the plains.

By the time Rocky Mountain National Park was established, after the turn of the century, all of the Indian tribes of Colorado had been settled on reservations. Their ultimate defeat and removal was the same throughout the West. Our stereotypical idea of the Indian, mounted on a horse and chasing bison, was a relatively short-lived culture that lasted at most 100 years. By the 1850s, white settlement and travel across the plains was beginning to infringe upon the traditional lifestyle of these tribes, and conflicts increased. With the discovery of gold in 1858, whites flooded into Colorado, and antagonism toward Indians increased. Indians occasionally killed settlers, and more often settlers killed Indians. The U.S. Army set up military posts throughout the West to provide protection for settlers and commerce over the Oregon Trail and other travel routes. Although the Indians won the occasional battle, they lost the war and eventually were removed from their land and confined to reservations. There were many sad and disgraceful massacres of Indian people by the U.S. military, such as the 1864 Sand Creek massacre in eastern Colorado, where 137 Cheyenne and Arapaho—109 of them women and children— were slaughtered in one day by Col. John Chivington, demonstrating to many Indian people that peace with the whites was unlikely.

Despite these occasional military battles, it wasn't the superior military power of the U.S. Army, but disease and starvation, that ultimately defeated the native people. As trade between whites and Indians increased, deadly diseases such as smallpox and tuberculosis were transmitted to native people, with disastrous consequences. Although these diseases killed many whites, they ravaged the native people, whose resistance to these European diseases was much lower. Often a third to half a tribe might die in a single major epidemic of these diseases. Tens of thousands more died from disease than were ever killed directly by settlers or the U.S. Army. As their numbers declined, tribes were more easily displaced from the best territories by their neighbors, further reducing their numbers.

Coupled with the disease was starvation. The bison herds that roamed the plains were the commissary for the tribes. One of the most popular trade items at trading posts was a bison hide. Trading post records show that Indian people killed hundreds of thousands, if not millions, of bison that were exchanged for rifles, blankets, and whiskey. By the 1850s, white buffalo hunters who pursued the bison herds relentlessly joined the tribes in this slaughter. By the 1870s, the annihilation of bison became an unwritten military policy. The army realized that if the bison were eliminated, the Indians would have no choice but to surrender and acquiesce to life on the reservation.

By the 1880s, the last large bison herds disappeared, and except for a few animals in Yellowstone and on a handful of private ranches, the millions of bison that once roamed the plains were virtually extirpated from the United States. The last wild Colorado bison was seen in Lost Park in 1897. With the loss of the bison, as predicted, the resolve of the Indian people was broken, and the last resistors were moved to reservations, often far from their traditional homes. Although they pleaded to be allowed to live on a reservation on the Cache la Poudre, in 1878 the Arapaho were moved northward to Wyoming and settled with their traditional enemies, the Shoshone, on the Shoshone-Arapaho Wind River Reservation. The Utes had fewer conflicts with settlers at first, but by the 1880s, they too were removed to reservations in western Colorado and northeast Utah.

The Reverend Elkanah Lamb, an early settler of Estes Park, expressed the sentiment of the times when he commented in his memoirs that the Indians "were an intolerable nuisance, always visiting our camps to buy, steal, and annoy." Of course, one could just as easily say the same about the whites and their treatment of the Indians.

Early Exploration and Settlement

As early as the late 1500s, Spanish military expeditions wandered north from Mexico into what would become the American Southwest. A territorial capital was established at Santa Fe, New Mexico. Expeditions sent northward from here are thought to have reached Colorado. In 1720, a Spanish force under the command of Don Pedro de Villasur, along with

100 men, traveled overland all the way to Nebraska. On their way back to Santa Fe, they were attacked by Pawnees on the South Fork of the Platte River, resulting in the death of eighty-eight Spanish. Although it is not recorded, no doubt the expedition members saw the Colorado Front Range from the South Fork of the Platte.

French fur trappers, who came from the east, were living among the Plains Indian tribes by the mid-1700s. Most of them left no written record, and it's unlikely that any ventured all the way to the mountains. Still, these traders knew of the existence of the Rockies.

The first American influence in the region came early in the 1800s. The United States had bought from France the vast Louisiana Purchase, which included the Front Range of Colorado. In 1806, Lt. Zebulon Pike, for whom Pikes Peak is named, penetrated Colorado and even crossed the Front Range into South Park. American fur trappers who traded with the Indians for beaver pelts soon followed Pike. Whether any of these trappers actually visited the site of Rocky Mountain National Park is not known, but certainly they were trapping all the rivers along the Front Range, including the Big Thompson and St. Vrain.

The next written record of contact with the region occurred in 1820, when Maj. Stephen Long mounted an expedition up the Platte River to the base of the Front Range. While still 100 miles from the mountains out on the plains, the expedition's journalist, Capt. John Bell, recorded seeing the Front Range of the Rockies. In particular, Bell noted in his journal (and quoted in the *Natural History of the Long Expedition to the Rocky Mountains*, by Howard E. Evans, Oxford University Press, 1997) that a "high peake was plainly to be distinguished towering above all the others as far as the sight extended." This high peak would later be named Longs Peak, after the expedition's leader. The Long Expedition had several French trappers as guides, and at least one of them had previously trapped in the mountains, supporting the notion that the French trappers were likely the first whites to penetrate the Colorado Rockies. After reaching the base of the Front Range, Long turned south, following the base of the mountains to present-day Colorado Springs. Here they climbed Pikes Peak and thence raced eastward along the Arkansas River to Fort Smith in Arkansas.

By the 1830s, the fur trade was in full swing, and trappers regularly wandered the Colorado Rockies. Trading posts were established on the plains near the mountain front, including Fort St. Vrain, Fort Lancaster,

Longs Peak is named for Maj. Stephen Long, who in 1820 led an expedition across the Great Plains to the base of the Rockies. Long never climbed his namesake peak, although he did ascend Pikes Peak to the south.

and Fort Jackson. All of them traded with the Indians and the occasional free trapper for beaver and bison pelts.

Rufus Sage, an adventurer and traveler, left Fort Lancaster in September 1843 and rode westward up into the mountains. Sage is thought to have been the first white to visit Estes Park, where he spent a month hunting. Sage noted that the area hosted an abundance of wildlife and mentioned the area's scenic beauty.

In 1858, gold was discovered in the Front Range, and the gold rush towns of Boulder, Denver, and Golden soon were home to thousands of eager and optimistic miners, camp followers, merchants, and prostitutes. One of these gold-seeking adventurers was Joe Estes. On a hunting trip in the mountains northeast of Denver, Estes and his son, Milton, stumbled onto the high mountain valley that later bore his name. Finding the valley inviting, they returned in 1860 to build a few cabins and begin a cattle operation in the well-water uplands. In addition to operating a cattle ranch, Estes hunted the abundant elk, bighorns, and deer of the mountains and sold them to miners in Denver and elsewhere. In one winter, they are reported to have killed 100 elk, plus bighorns, deer, and antelope.

In August 1864, William Byers, editor of *Rocky Mountain News*, set out with several companions to visit Estes Park. They visited with Estes and his family, and then Byers and friends attempted a climb of Longs Peak. They failed to find a suitable route to the summit, but they did climb Mount Meeker. From that high eminence, Byers looked at Longs Peak and predicted that no one would ever reach the summit. Although the thousands of people who have climbed Longs Peak since then have proven him wrong, Byers was correct when he suggested "eventually this park will become a favorite pleasure resort."

In August 1868, Byers joined John Wesley Powell, who later went on to become the first person to run the Colorado River, in another attempt on the peak. Byers, Powell, and five others left a base camp on Grand Lake and rode horses up into the mountains as far they could go. They left their horses and proceeded on foot, eventually finding a passable route to the summit. They spent three hours on the summit enjoying the view, then descended, spending a cold night on the mountain without food before they could reach their horses and return to their base camp.

Estes Park is a mountain-flanked valley named for Joe Estes, who settled here in 1860 to hunt big game to sell to miners and raise cattle.

The lure of this high summit soon prompted others to follow in their footsteps. In 1873, Ferdinand Hayden, leader of one of the first government exploratory expeditions in the Yellowstone region, ascended the peak with Anna Dickinson, the first woman to successfully climb the peak. A month later, Isabella Bird, an adventurous Englishwoman, also climbed the peak, guided by a local called Rocky Mountain Jim. Bird stayed in the valley for five months and described her time in Estes Park in letters home to her sister, which eventually were collected and published in her book, *A Lady's Life in the Rocky Mountains*.

Around this same time, a wealthy English aristocrat named Windham Thomas Wynham-Quin, the earl of Dunraven, visited Estes Park. In 1871, the earl hunted bison, deer, and elk with Buffalo Bill Cody along Wyoming's North Platte River. In 1872, he was back in the West, visiting Colorado's South Park, among other areas. While in Denver, the earl heard tales of Estes Park. He visited Estes Park and hunted elk along the Fall River and Bear Lake areas, and left with a favorable impression of the mountain valley and its abundance of game. In 1873, the earl returned to Estes Park. He was smitten, and decided he had to own the valley. Most of the land was still public domain but available to homesteading. Using a common ploy of the day, the earl hired men to file on 160-acre homesteads around the valley. After they had gained title to the plots from the government, the earl purchased them. In this manner, he was eventually able to amass more than 8,200 acres in the valley.

The earl used his holdings as a summer retreat and cattle ranch. By the summer of 1877, he had expanded his business ventures to include an elegant hotel to cater to the ever-increasing demands of sophisticated tourists already beginning to discover the delights of Estes Park. The earl was not the only one tapping into the growing tourist business. Nearly all of the other early settlers occasionally housed guests to earn extra cash, and some soon made it a full-time occupation. Estes Park was already on its way toward becoming a tourist-based economy.

Mining Minerals

While the earl and others were mining the growing number of tourists in Estes Park, mineral discoveries in the Never Summer Range and along the North Fork of the Colorado were fueling a minor rush to Grand Lake and the surrounding region. In 1879, four prospectors found promising ore on the North Fork of the Colorado, and Lulu City was born. By 1881, the town boosted more than forty houses plus assorted businesses, includ-

The Jim Shipler cabin, on the North Fork of the Colorado, is a relict of the mining era, when Lulu City and other short-lived communities sprang up to provide for the needs of miners. Shipler, with three companions, discovered a silver claim on Shipler Mountain.

ing hardware, several grocery, and liquor stores. Mining continued in the region, and the future seemed promising. Though the ore contained some minerals, the distance to a smelter precluded development. By 1883, Lulu City was losing population, and by 1886, all of the mining operations in the North Fork Valley had ceased operations. The short-lived mining boom came to an end. It is fortunate that mining failed in the region, for had there been substantial mineralization, almost certainly what is now Rocky Mountain National Park never would have been set aside.

Enos Mills and the Park Movement

If you look closely at the history of almost any national park, there usually were one or more key figures who had a vision and kept that vision always in the forefront of their lives. Yosemite had John Muir. Olympic National Park owes its existence to Willard Van Name and the Emergency Conservation Committee. We can thank Marjorie Stoneman Douglas for the Everglades.

More than any other person, Rocky Mountain National Park is a monument to the efforts of Enos Mills, an Estes Park naturalist, guide, mountaineer, hotel owner, and park advocate. Mills's life was intertwined with the park and was emblematic of the changing attitudes of the American experience, where conquering nature and the frontier changed to one of greater respect and care for natural landscapes. Since Mills was so intricately tied to the creation of Rocky Mountain National Park, it is worth looking at his life story in some detail.

Mills was born in 1870, just two years before Yellowstone became our first national park. He grew up in Kansas but was a sickly boy. At this time, the "healthful" air of the Rockies was being promoted as a cure for all kinds of ailments. Seeking relief from his health problems, Mills left his family when just fourteen to move to Estes Park, Colorado, then still a small community of less than 150. Mills found work at the Elkhorn Lodge, one of the early venues catering to tourists, and immediately began to explore the surrounding mountains. This early exposure to a tourist-based economy influenced Mills in future years. He often used tourism to justify establishment of Rocky Mountain National Park.

Never one to shirk work, Mills always earned his own way. He did, however, decide early on that work should not be for work's sake alone, and he always sought out jobs that provided adventure, or at least paid high enough wages so that he could spend part of each year outdoors exploring wildlands. For the next three summers, he continued to work for various lodges in Estes Park while exploring the area in his free time. In 1885, his second summer in Colorado, he climbed Longs Peak, the first of 304 ascents of the mountain. After this first climb, he determined to make guiding tourists his occupation. But it took a while before the fifteen-year-old boy could establish himself in the tourist trade. Neverthe-

Longs Peak, seen here in winter through aspen, was climbed more than 304 times by Enos Mills, including the first winter ascent. Mills is often known as the "father" of Rocky Mountain National Park for his ceaseless efforts to establish a national park in the Estes Park region.

less, he began to put down roots in the Estes Park area by building a cabin in the valley, thus establishing his ties to the Rockies.

In 1887, seeking to earn higher wages than ranching or working in a lodge offered, Mills went north to the booming mining community of Butte, Montana, where he got the first of many high-paying seasonal jobs. For the next fifteen years, Mills continued to work summers guiding tourists and winters in the mining industry. In between jobs, he roamed the mountains on his own.

A pivotal event that changed his life occurred in the fall of 1889. Mills returned to Butte, again seeking employment in the mines, but underground fires temporarily closed the mining operations. Mills decided to visit California. While walking on a beach in San Francisco's Golden Gate Park, he chanced to meet the conservationist and Sierra Club founder John Muir. Muir was deeply engrossed in a conversation with a group of people. As the crowd dispersed, Mills approached Muir, and soon they were discussing their mutual interest in conservation and nature.

Muir was then fifty years old, already a well-known national conservation figure involved in the debate over establishing the Yosemite region as a national park. After hearing Mills's tales of explorations in the Rockies, Muir encouraged the young man to pursue a life as a wildlands advocate. For the rest of his life, Mills held Muir up as a role model and attributed this chance meeting to having provided a focus for his life. He wrote, "I owe everything to Muir. If it hadn't been for him, I would have been a mere gypsy."

In between jobs, Mills continued to explore the wilds of Colorado and also ventured farther afield, traveling to the Sierra Nevada, Yellowstone, Alaska, and Europe. He soon developed an almost legendary reputation for daring exploits. He regularly scaled peaks in winter, slept out without a tent in snowstorms, and spent weeks at a time hiking and camping by himself in the wilderness. All this time in the outdoors gave him ample opportunity to become a keen observer of the natural world and growing fame as a first-rate self-taught naturalist. By 1902, he had purchased a lodge in Estes Park, becoming an innkeeper and guide. The Longs Peak Inn, as he named it, gave him ample opportunities to discuss his knowledge of the natural world with responsive audiences, and he soon had a large clientele, including such famous guests as Eugene Debs, Douglas Fairbanks, Clarence Darrow, and William Allen White.

After buying the lodge, he gave up mining. Instead, in 1903, he obtained a winter job as a snow surveyor. His job was to measure snow depths so that predictions about runoff for irrigation could be calculated. It was the perfect job for Mills. Alone, he traipsed across Colorado's mountains on snowshoes, daring blizzards and relishing the winter solitude. He even made the first winter ascent of Longs Peak.

In 1905, following in the footsteps of John Muir, Mills wrote a book describing Estes Park, the first of fifteen books he would write in his career. All of his books had an abundance of natural history observation, demonstrating Mills's keen abilities as a naturalist. But they also had a considerable amount of self-aggrandizement as well, with Mills seeming almost larger than life as he rides avalanches down mountains, clings to windswept icy slopes with fingernails, and experiences numerous close encounters with grizzly bears. Armchair readers at the turn of the century found Mills's adventures fascinating, and he soon had a devoted following of admirers. As was the tradition of the times, he also began to travel extensively as a public speaker, telling tales of his adventures in the Rockies.

Mills's conservation ethic was growing as well, and increasingly his message included advocacy for wildlands protection. In 1907, President Theodore Roosevelt hired Mills as a spokesperson for Gifford Pinchot's Forest Service, giving Mills an even greater platform from which to advocate for forest protection. This gave him greater national exposure and a growing reputation as a conservationist.

During this same period, throughout the 1890s and into the new century, there was a growing conservation movement in America that sought to slow or stop the rapacious squandering of natural resources that had characterized the frontier era. In general, the government policy toward public domain was to get rid of these lands as quickly as possible. Throughout the 1800s, the federal government gave away huge chunks of land to homesteaders, miners, loggers, railroads, states, and just about anyone who would or could take or use the land for some kind of resource exploitation. The goal was to get public lands into private hands as expeditiously as possible. The designation of Yellowstone National Park in 1872, withdrawing these lands from development and privatization, was a rare exception to government policy. But this attitude was changing. As the frontier era ended, more and more Americans supported the notion that at least some lands should be retained in public ownership and protected from development.

In 1890, Muir and others successfully lobbied to establish Yosemite and Sequoia National Parks. This was followed a year later with a proclamation by President Benjamin Harrison that withdrew 13 million acres of federal land from the public domain and set them aside as forest reserves, forerunners of our national forests. A few years later, in 1897, President

Grover Cleveland established another 21 million acres as forest reserves. The acts creating the forest reserves did not specify that exploitation was permitted. Muir, who viewed the forest reserve as just another form of national park, was delighted, but western resource extraction interests were outraged. Almost immediately, the mining, grazing, and logging interests began to lobby to repeal Cleveland's reserves. Within months, they had rallied their forces and successfully passed the Forest Management Act, which, among other things, specifically stated that forest reserves would be open to logging, mining, and grazing.

The Forest Management Act created a split in the young conservation movement. Preservationists like John Muir realized that forest reserves left little room for protection of wild nature, and he advocated the creation of additional national parks as a means of preserving undeveloped landscapes. This put him squarely at odds with Gifford Pinchot, a wealthy young forester who advocated utilization goals for public lands and who would later become the first director of the U.S. Forest Service.

Initially, Muir and Pinchot were friends and allies in the struggle to retain public control of the public domain. For his day, Pinchot was a progressive voice for the wise use of natural resources. This philosophy eventually put him at odds with John Muir, who felt that livestock grazing was one of the most destructive activities occurring in the mountains of the West. It was with great agitation that Muir learned in 1897 that Pinchot had decided to support sheep grazing on forest reserve lands. Muir, after reading Pinchot's endorsement of grazing on forest reserves, confronted him in a Seattle hotel lobby. When Pinchot acknowledged that he supported grazing as a legitimate use of forest reserves, Muir broke off his relationship with him. This split symbolized a division within the conservation movement that exists to this day between those who believe that humans have not only the knowledge to manage the land, but the willpower to do so wisely, and those who believe that such attitudes are arrogant and unsupported by the facts.

Against this backdrop of national politics, there was some local support in Colorado for protecting the Front Range from excess resource exploitation. As early as 1892, John Coy of Fort Collins proposed the creation of a forest reserve for the headwaters of the St. Vrain, Big Thompson, and Cache la Poudre Rivers. Opposition to the idea quickly developed, and the plan faded away, but it was not forgotten.

Enos Mills cabin.

With the election of ardent outdoor enthusiast and naturalist Theodore Roosevelt to the presidency, conservationists found a receptive ear in Washington. Roosevelt quickly expanded the forest reserve system. Among other areas, Roosevelt protected the Estes Park region in Colorado as part of the Medicine Bow Forest Reserve in 1905. In the same year, administration for the forest reserves was transferred to the Department of Agriculture and came under the newly created U.S. Forest Service, headed by Gifford Pinchot. Pinchot renamed the reserves national forests. In 1907, headquarters for the Medicine Bow Forest Reserve, later named the Colorado National Forest, was established in Estes Park.

After watching cattle trample wildflowers in the mountain meadows around Estes Park, Mills, like Muir, found that the newly created national forests did not provide legal protection for wild landscapes. By 1908, Enos Mills gave up on his support of national forests and, again like Muir, turned to national parks to protect the wildlands he loved. He began to advocate for the creation of a national park for the region. In his book *Rocky Mountain Wonderland,* he wrote, "Though a Forest Reserve, like a farm, has beauty, it is not established for its beauty but for practical purposes." He went on to say: "Trees to the forester mean what cattle do to the butcher. Lumber is his product and to recite 'Woodsman, spare that tree' to a forester would be like asking the butcher to spare the ox." He argued, "If scenery is to be saved, it must be saved for its own sake, on its own merits; it cannot be saved as something incidental."

To save a vestige of wildlands in the Colorado Rockies, Mills proposed a park twenty-four miles from north to south and forty-two miles from east to west, focused on the Estes Park area. Although there is no doubt that Mills was seeking to protect wildlands and wildlife, he was effective in promoting parks as an economic development tool. Parks, he wrote in *Rocky Mountain Wonderland*, "are not a luxury but a profitable investment." He compared the Rockies to the Alps and complained that the United States was behind most nations in making profitable use of scenery. "Alpine scenery annually produces upward of ten thousand dollars to the square mile, while the Rocky Mountains are being despoiled by cattle and sawmills for a few dollars a square mile." Despite his economic arguments, Mills recognized that parks also had spiritual value to Americans. He suggested that without parks, "all that is best in civilization will be smothered." Indeed, Mills came to believe that parks represented everything good in the world and were an antidote for all of society's ills.

Mills soon had the support of the Estes Park Protective and Improvement Association. In 1911, the organization approved support for a Rocky Mountain National Park. Other organizations, including the Denver Chamber of Commerce and American Civic Association, endorsed the park proposal. But not everyone was supportive. The U.S. Forest Service strongly opposed the park, fearing a loss of influence over western lands. A group of Estes Park residents and landowners formed the Front Range Settlers League to advocate for private-property rights and minimal government control. To anyone knowledgeable with western public land issues of today, all of these basic philosophical perspectives are quite familiar.

By 1913, a bill to create Rocky Mountain National Park was introduced into Congress. Opposition continued to mount, and the size of Mills's park proposal shrank. Support, for instance, from the Colorado Mountain Club was based on the fact that the shrunken park boundaries effectively excluded any lands that had real value for extractive industries. The proposed boundaries carefully avoided the best timberlands, grazing lands, and mineralized belts. Rocky Mountain National Park was largely a "rocks and ice" park. Such politically based boundaries that avoided biological realities later came back to haunt park supporters. Nevertheless, in 1913, even the emaciated park proposal was not certain of Congressional approval, and the first and second efforts at passage of a park bill failed.

Mills and others continued to lobby for the park. In their efforts, they were joined by a growing chorus of supporters from across the country. Such national publications as *Atlantic Monthly*, *Collier's*, *Saturday Evening Post*, *Forest and Stream*, and *National Geographic* all supported the park proposal. Mills even corresponded with John Muir during the park campaign, garnering support and encouragement from his mentor. Muir died in December 1914, just months before the park legislation cleared its final hurdles and became a reality. On January 26, 1915, President Woodrow Wilson signed into law a bill creating Rocky Mountain National Park.

F. O. Stanley, inventor of the Stanley Steamer, an early automobile, opened up the Stanley Hotel in 1909. Stanley, along with Mills, was a staunch national park supporter.

Although the final legislation created a park one-third as large as Mills had originally proposed, the park establishment was still a major political success. For Mills, it was the high point of his career, and his contribution to the park creation was dutifully acknowledged when the *Denver Post* declared that Mills was "The Father of Rocky Mountain National Park."

The Park Service Takes Over

In 1915, when Rocky Mountain National Park was created, there were thirty-one national parks, including Glacier, Crater Lake, Sequoia, Yosemite, Mount Rainier, Mesa Verde, and General Grant. Nevertheless, there was no agency responsible for the administration of this growing system of parks, and management varied from unit to unit. To oversee this expanding array of park units, Congress created the National Park Service in 1916. Stephen Mather, a wealthy Chicago businessman who loved national parks, was appointed in 1917 as its first director. Mather was a tireless park promoter and was generous with his wealth, paying for everything from the purchase of the Tioga Road in Yosemite Park to the salary of the national park publicist.

In 1917, Mills published his book *Your National Parks,* which waxed favorably about Stephen Mather and parks. In previous articles, he had praised Mather as an outdoor lover and described him as "calm yet enthusiastic." Yet less than two years later, he was denouncing Mather and the agency.

Mills's first complaint was the timid way the Park Service approached potential expansions. Less than two years after Rocky Mountain National Park was established, it was enlarged to take in the Twin Sisters, Deer Mountain, and other areas. But Mills also advocated expansion south of the park to include the Indian Peaks region, the Never Summer Range to the west, and the Mount Evans area west of Denver. The Park Service, not wanting to antagonize regional opponents, chose instead to lobby for more modest additions.

Mills might have forgiven the Park Service for a lack of courage, particularly in the face of strong political opposition, but a new park policy instituted by Stephen Mather turned Mills, one of the young agency's resolute supporters, into a determined and bitter critic of the agency. Mather, hoping to create better-organized service for tourists, granted exclusive monopolies to companies operating concessions in the parks. Mather justified the monopolies, claiming that the companies would invest in park developments only if they knew they were guaranteed exclusive privileges. He also believed that allowing only a few companies to run various services in the parks would reduce the need for multiple offices, garages, and other development. Exclusive franchises also provided the Park Service a degree of control over park development, since they could dictate the kind and style of development that would be permitted. For instance, Mather demanded that all construction maintain rustic architectural styles that would blend with the "primitive" appeal of the parks. Mather's actions not only outraged Mills and others at Rocky Mountain National Park, but created antagonism among users and supporters of other parks as well.

In 1919, Mather gave the Roe Emery Rocky Mountain Park Transportation Company the exclusive contract for all public transportation in the park. Anyone entering the park in a commercial vehicle, including people staying at lodges within the park, had to travel in a Roe Emery vehicle.

Early ranchers and miners soon learned that they could earn more money mining tourists. The Never Summer Ranch was built in 1918 and, with the opening of the Fall River Road across the Continental Divide, became a dude ranch providing accommodations to an ever-increasing tide of tourists. In 1973, the ranch was sold. It was eventually bought by the National Park Service.

Mills, according to his biographer Alexander Drummond, incensed by Mather's new policies, wrote, "All the resources of these parks, which afford a living to numerous resident local people, are given out to monopolies, over which the public have no control and which the public cannot remove." In granting these monopolies, Mather was validating the worst fears of park opponents, such as the Front Range Settlers League, who had fought the park because they viewed "with concern and alarm the possibility of trade and traffic privileges farmed out and licensed to strangers by a park administration." Now Mills had to acknowledge that his opponents' rhetoric had been right after all.

The new policy also had a direct economic effect upon Mills, since his Longs Peak Inn lay within the park, as did eight other hotels. All were not permitted to transport guests from Estes Park to their establishments without using Emery vehicles. But the personal economic inconvenience was minor compared with how Mather's new policies upset Mills's strong sense of fairness. To a man who grow up with Standard Oil control of petroleum and who had witnessed how the Anaconda Mining Company had taken over and dominated the political machinery and media of Montana, Mather's endorsed monopolies seemed to Mills to be a direct threat to democracy. Mills claimed that the Emery Company not only put many local tour operators out of business, but also charged higher rates than had been the case when free market competition existed. Mills was angered by excessive profits enjoyed by these park monopolies: "Why should private concerns reap profits by exploiting the visitors to National Parks?"

To test the Park Service's resolve, Mills sent a car from his lodge on a tour of the park, and as expected, the park superintendent, Claude Way, ordered the vehicle to leave the park. Mills eventually filed a suit against the Park Service, claiming they interfered with his "common right as a citizen of Colorado in traveling over Park roads." The Park Service, for its part, tried to reach a compromise with Mills, offering to allow him and other lodge owners the right to transport their own guests to and from their inns. But principle, not economics, was at stake with Mills, and he continued to fight the park policies. The U.S. attorney managed to get the judge to dismiss the case.

The legal setback didn't prevent Mills and others from provoking another confrontation. Mills and other tour operations continued to drive in the park, hoping to force the Park Service to arrest them, but the agency, not wishing to have a major test case come up before the courts, did not enforce its regulations. Nevertheless, one of the jitney drivers, Charles Robins, filed another suit against the Park Service, claiming they violated his right to travel freely. In his suit, he was soon joined by the state of Colorado. Robins eventually lost his suit, but the entire controversy had damaged the Park Service's reputation and the morale of its employees. Tired of enforcing an unpopular policy, Superintendent Way resigned.

When the lawsuits failed, Mills continued his attacks in the media, writing numerous critical articles and giving impassioned speeches to all who would listen. As his bitterness grew over the loss of his and others' court cases, Mills's rhetoric became incendiary and full of hyperbole. He denounced Mather's policies as sweeping totalitarianism, comparing the Park Service director to the German Kaiser and calling the agency a "Prussianized Park System." Others shared Mills's sense of outrage. Free-lan Stanley, inventor of the Stanley Steamer and owner of the Stanley Hotel, once a staunch park supporter, now denounced the Park Service's policies. Stanley claimed that in the nineteen years he had lived in Estes Park, he had contributed more than $55,000 for the construction of roads that his tour buses were now denied the full use of.

But many of Mills's old supporters began to question his wisdom and motives. They argued that the Park Service was already under attack from critics who didn't want to see any lands set aside as parks, and Mills, by continuously attacking Mather and the agency, was undermining the entire concept of parks. Horace McFarland, a strong park supporter and friend of Mills, tried to talk Mills into softening his rhetoric, suggesting that his continual diatribes against the park might jeopardize the entire park system. McFarland wrote, "It is about the worst time that ever has occurred for a sane man who loves the parks as you do, to slam them because of incidental inequity you have discovered in their management." But Mills merely attacked his critics and was unable to look beyond the issue, probably hurting the prospects for future parks in the process.

On a speaking trip to New York in the winter of 1922, Mills fell and broke a rib in a subway. The injury, combined with the stress of his seemingly hopeless battle against a bureaucracy, weakened his normally strong constitution. Throughout the spring and summer, his condition did not improve, and a long-standing battle with a neighbor who continually

grazed his cows on the meadows about Mills's lodge added to his aggrava-
tion and worry. Then, on September 20, after mingling with guests at his
lodge, he went to bed, woke up in the early-morning hours in pain, and
died before dawn of blood poisoning at age fifty-one.

Though Mills may have exaggerated the consequences of park monopolies, the debate over park concessionaires has continued to be an ongoing
and never-ending battle for environmentalists in many different national
parks around the country. It is unfortunate that Mills was unable to enjoy
the park he had worked so long and hard to establish. His final years were
marred by bitterness toward the agency for which he had once held such
high hopes, and which he viewed as having hindered the reality of his
dream of an ideal, protected wildlands, which he had made the focus of
his entire adult life.

Park Management Controversies

The death of Mills eliminated one of the agency's most vocal and articu-
late critics, and within a few years, the monopoly issue was eliminated
when Congress passed legislation granting the agency the authority to
implement such policies. Though concessionaire monopolies in Rocky
Mountain National Park were no longer an issue, the Park Service still
faced other controversies.

Mather and the agency he managed felt that maximizing tourist enjoyment was the only way to ensure continued public support for the parks.
To this end, they instituted practices that today the agency would frown
upon, if not outright condemn. Fishing was always a popular activity in
the parks, and yet much of Rocky Mountain National Park waters were so
high and isolated that they did not hold any native fish. Fish, particularly
trout, were stocked across the landscape without regard for the existing
fish populations or protection of aquatic ecosystems.

Rangers also felt it was necessary to lure wildlife to places where visitors could easily encounter them. To this end, salt blocks were placed in
strategic locations to bring wildlife close to the roads. One government
official even suggested building fenced enclosures to create an outdoor
zoo to display the park's larger wildlife.

At the same time the agency was promoting "good" animals, such as
deer, elk, and bighorn sheep, it was eliminating the "bad" animals, generally those species that preyed upon deer, elk, and bighorn sheep, such as
mountain lions, wolves, coyotes, and other predators.

Trail Creek Road was constructed between 1929 and 1933 and is considered one of the most scenic drives in the United States.

To encourage greater use of the park, Rocky Mountain National Park embarked on a development program that included the construction of the Fall River Road, which enabled visitors to cross the Continental Divide by vehicle. Campgrounds and trails were constructed. And the ranger-naturalist program was developed, with rangers leading tourists on hikes and giving campfire talks in the evening. The park's tourist promotion worked better than anyone ever dreamed. In the first year after the park's establishment, 50,000 people visited Rocky Mountain National Park. Just four years later, in 1920, visitation had jumped to 240,966 people.

To manage the influx of tourists, more ranger housing and hotels had to be constructed. In the mid-1920s, the Park Service began to lobby for an appropriation from Congress to construct the Trail Creek Road. Funds for the scenic highway were finally appropriated in 1929, and the new road was opened for visitor use in 1933. The Trail Ridge Road was billed as a new "scenic wonder of the world." Trail Creek Road joined other Park Service scenic highways, including the Blue Ridge Parkway in North Carolina and Virginia, Cape Royal Road in Grand Canyon, Round the Mountain Road at Mount Rainier, Going to the Sun Highway in Glacier, and others constructed to allow the motoring public greater access to park vistas. These roads had their desired effect. From a total of 292,000 tourists in 1933, when the Trail Ridge Road was opened for use, in 1938 more than 660,000 people visited Rocky Mountain National Park.

Attracting people in summer was easy, but both the agency and local business leaders were eager to draw tourists in winter as well. Beginning in the 1930s, interest in skiing grew throughout the Rockies. By 1941, a primitive rope tow was installed in Hidden Valley, and by the 1950s, several T-bars and a lodge were constructed on the site.

In the 1950s, the growing popularity of the parks in the postwar years led to a deterioration of facilities made for a time of slow-paced travel and fewer visitors. Park facilities, roads, and resources were all in disrepair. In response, the Park Service developed their Mission 66 program, something like a Marshall Plan for the parks. The agency asked Congress for a massive infusion of funds to repair and expand development. In 1956, Congress provided more than $1 billion for park upgrades and repairs, providing much-needed funds to Rocky Mountain National Park and other national park units. Mission 66 accomplished its goal, and many park facilities were upgraded or improved.

But this rash of development did nothing to quell a growing perception among many conservationists that the Park Service appeared to care more about providing recreational opportunities than preserving nature. In Rocky Mountain National Park and elsewhere, the Park Service's tendency to promote development worried wildland advocates, and as early as the 1930s, some organizations, such as the Wilderness Society and the Sierra Club, began to shift their support from the Park Service to the Forest Service as the best keepers of wildlands. Despite the boom in construction, the Park Service informally held to a policy of keeping large areas of the parks in a natural condition, while concentrating use and people in a few corridors and locations.

While the national parks were attempting to entice more visitors, Rocky Mountain National Park began to discuss potential park expansion ideas. Superintendent Roger Toll, who replaced Superintendent Way, began to lobby for expansion of the park to include Arapaho Glacier to the south and the Never Summer Range to the west, both of which were then under National Forest administration. Opponents claimed that a larger park would jeopardize jobs in logging, grazing, and mining industries, voicing the usual argument against expansion. In the face of grow-ing opposition, the Park Service backed down on its expansion proposals.

Fueling the local opposition was the issue of roads and their con-trols. People were angry not only because all commercial activities were restricted to a few chosen operators, but also because the agency began to charge an admission fee for park entrance. To locals who had had free access to the resources on federal lands and wanted to use them merely for hiking and camping, paying an entrance fee was an encroachment on the rights and property of American citizens.

Fear of a federal takeover was also fueled by the Park Service's desire to acquire private inholdings in the park. Inholdings not only created con-flicts among park users, the agency, and private landowners, but it also could interfere with park management policies; for example, a desire to allow fires to burn would be hampered by private inholdings. Starting almost immediately after the park was established, the agency began to purchase private inholdings as they became available. Most landowners were willing to sell to the agency, and by 1963, Rocky Mountain National Park had acquired more than 11,000 acres. As recently as 1990, the park was expanded to include Lily Lake area.

Restoration of these lands often eliminated nearly all trace of these for-mer dwellings. For example, the Stead Ranch in Moraine Park, which was purchased in 1962, included barns, cabins, a lodge, and even a golf course, all of which are gone today. Indeed, most people driving through the naturalized Moraine Park would never guess that it was once a small com-munity of ranches and cabins. Despite what one may hear about crowding and damage to the park from too many visitors, perspective is needed. In many ways, Rocky Mountain National Park has less development than it did forty years ago.

A legal handle for preserving the natural landscape from incremental development came with the passage of the 1964 Wilderness Act. The act provided a mechanism for creating a national system of wilderness areas that would be managed to retain their natural qualities. Federal lands that were essentially undeveloped were to be studied by federal agencies including the Forest Service, Bureau of Land Management, Fish and Wildlife Service, and the Park Service to determine which lands had qualities that would qualify them for inclusion in the national wilder-ness system. The Wilderness Act finally gave the parks a legal mandate

Cabins, lodges, and even a golf course once littered Moraine Park. Gradually the National Park Service has acquired these lands and restored the landscape to near pristine condition.

not only to provide for recreation, but also to preserve natural landscapes themselves.

After spending years studying the issue, in the early 1970s, Rocky Mountain National Park finally released its recommendations for wilderness. The agency found that approximately 90 percent of Rocky Mountain National Park had wilderness qualities as defined by the Wilderness Act. Public hearings were held, and a majority of those responding supported protection of the park wildlands. In 1976, final recommendations proposed 235,668 acres of the park's total 265,193 acres as wilderness. Congress has yet to design these acres as official wilderness; nevertheless, Rocky Mountain National Park manages these lands so as not to compromise their wildland qualities.

Transporting water from the western slope of the Rockies to the parched eastern slope was always an attractive idea to farmers and communities on the eastern side. As early as 1890, the first of many water projects in what

Skier views Wild Basin, one of the more remote parts of the park. The majority of Rocky Mountain National Park was found to have wilderness qualities and is managed to keep it roadless and undeveloped.

would become Rocky Mountain National Park was begun. The Grand Ditch, still easily visible to visitors on Trail Ridge Road, was designed to capture snowmelt in the Never Summer Range and transport it to the headwaters of the Cache la Poudre, where it would augment that river's flow, making more water available for irrigation on the plains. The project proceeded slowly, since most of the work was done by hand and, given the high elevation, could be done only during a very short summer season. It was not until 1936 that the final segment of the 14.3-mile ditch was completed to Baker Creek.

Storing water in the Rockies for use on the plains soon became a major source of antagonism between conservationists and development interests. In nearly all instances, the conservationists lost. The largest of these developments is the Colorado–Big Thompson Project. As early as 1905, people were looking longingly toward the Colorado River headwaters as a potential water source for irrigation projects on the plains. In anticipation of some kind of transdivide water development, the federal Bureau of Reclamation (BOR) claimed lands about Grand Lake for water diversion projects. When Rocky Mountain National Park was established in 1915, the BOR was assured that any water projects it might propose would not be obstructed by the designation of the park.

In 1933, the idea for a tunnel to be drilled under the Continental Divide from Grand Lake to the Wind River was unveiled. The Park Service fought the proposal from the beginning. They argued that commercial extractive activities had no place in a national park and that power lines, tunnels, reservoirs, and turbines would mar the values for which the park was established. Numerous environmental groups soon joined the Park Service in their opposition to the proposed project. But then as now, farmers carried far more political power than their numbers might suggest, and they were easily able to overwhelm conservationists and the Park Service.

The package was difficult to stop. Supporters of the tunnel promised water for agriculture, hydroelectric power for cities, and jobs for everyone—a very enticing promise in the Depression era. In 1937, President Franklin Roosevelt signed the legislation authorizing the project. By 1944, the 13.1-mile-long tunnel was completed. By 1947, Colorado River water was flowing across the Divide and down to the plains to grow hay, corn, and other commodities already being produced in excess quantities without irrigation elsewhere in the United States.

Shadow Mountain Lake, in the Arapaho National Recreation Area. The lake is part of a water-storage system that transports Colorado River water across the Continental Divide via a 13.1-mile-long tunnel dug through the mountains.

Despite the fact that the Park Service fought against some development, such as dams and water development, and even was beginning to restore some parts of the park that had previously been grazed by domestic livestock, used for lodges, or even as golf courses or ski areas, there was still criticism that Rocky Mountain National Park was mismanaging the natural landscape of the park. Such assertions sometimes failed to consider historical circumstances or were the result of the misinterpretation of evidence. The two biggest controversies are wildfire (discussed in some detail in the plant chapter) and the management of wildlife such as elk and deer.

The controversy in Rocky Mountain National Park over elk and deer is significant, because its implications go well beyond this particular park. It is part of a much larger ongoing debate that has waxed and waned for decades over the appropriate level of human manipulation in natural systems and, in particular, how best to manage or not manage populations of elk, deer, and other large ungulates. The same debates are occurring in Grand Teton, Yellowstone, Mount Rainier, and Olympic, among other parks. There is no agreement over how to deal with ungulate populations.

The issue of ungulate abundance hinges partially on historic accounts. There is an abundance of evidence suggesting that historic populations of elk, deer, and other big game attracted humans to the Estes Park region. Indians journeyed to the mountains to hunt some animals, such as bighorns and elk, and the first white settlers and trappers in the region all remarked on the abundance of big game. The earl of Dunraven and other sportsmen flocked to the region to hunt elk, deer, bighorn sheep, and bears. Joe Estes made his living supplying miners with elk and deer he killed near his ranch in the valley. Enos Mills reported numerous encounters with wild bighorns, elk, and other wildlife during his rambles of the mountains.

Some suggest that this observed abundance of wildlife was a historic anomaly. Others suggest that heavy hunting pressure from Native Americans kept big-game numbers to very low levels. But when introduced diseases decimated Indian populations, decreased pressure on big game allowed them to reach unnaturally high numbers.

Still, wildlife abundance is what early settlers thought was the norm. And this is the standard on which subsequent wildlife management was based. Unregulated hunting, combined with excessive competition with livestock, led to huge declines in big-game herds. By 1900, elk were nearly extirpated throughout the state. By 1912, it was estimated that fewer than a dozen elk resided on the entire Roosevelt National Forest and Rocky Mountain National Park. By the turn of the century, the only place left with sizable elk herds was Yellowstone Park. The same thing was true of mule deer. Deer were so rare that some western papers would give a sighting of a live deer front-page status.

In response to this decline in wildlife numbers, many states enacted strict hunting and fishing regulations, in many cases outlawing hunting for some species altogether. In addition, predators were zealously hunted down throughout the West, even trapped and shot in national parks. Rocky Mountain National Park was no exception. By the 1920s, most biologists considered mountain lions, wolves, and grizzly bears to be extinct in Rocky Mountain National Park. Though the Park Service reversed its stand on predators and began to protect them by 1926, by then many of the larger predators were already extirpated. Freedom from predators helped hasten the restoration of big-game animal numbers.

At the time, efforts to restore favored wildlife species such as elk to suitable habitat were undertaken. In 1913 and 1914, 49 elk from Yellowstone Park were transplanted to Estes Park. By 1921, this small nucleus of elk had risen to 120 animals, and there were more than 300 animals by 1930. With just 300 animals, some biologists were reporting that Rocky Mountain National Park had too many elk, a refrain that would be repeated for the next sixty years.

The first annual spring wildlife report opined that the range was in "very poor condition because of overuse." Much of this use was from domestic livestock, which were grazed on much of the lower-elevation terrain in Estes Park still in private hands, as well as from the horses used by the numerous dude ranches and lodges that were inholdings within the park. This grazing pressure left little for elk to eat in the winter months, and serious debarking of aspen was reported at this time. Elk eat the bark of aspen when deep snow hides grasses and other food. This prompted the Park Service to acquire additional winter range for elk and deer, including parcels in Beaver Meadow, Horseshoe Park, and part of Moraine Park, and to remove livestock competition. By 1932, the only livestock grazing remaining was in Moraine Park.

Despite these measures, some biologists continued to report what they considered to be declining range condition. Park Service biologist Joseph Dixon stated as early as 1931 that he felt the park supported excess elk and deer populations that needed to be reduced. Dixon drew this same conclusion in a 1939 report on Rocky Mountain National Park range condition, noting that there were 900 elk in the park and that the carrying

Elk graze above the Cache la Poudre River. Market and subsistence hunting had so decimated elk in the region that elk from Yellowstone National Park were released in Estes Park to reestablish herds here.

capacity of the winter range had been exceeded. The superintendent of the park came to different conclusions, however, stating in 1938 that the elk were in good condition and there was no immediate forage problem.

Rocky Mountain National Park wasn't the only place where some people, both in and outside the Park Service, were complaining about excess elk and deer. In Yellowstone, critics were complaining that the park was being devastated by its elk and would soon be a barren wasteland. Indeed, by 1935, rangers in Yellowstone were shooting elk to reduce their population to what was deemed to be an acceptable number. The first year, rangers and hunters outside the park killed over 3,300 elk on Yellowstone's northern range. Still, there were eminent biologists who opposed the direct reduction policy, including University of California–Berkeley wildlife professor Joseph Grinnell, who urged the Park Service to submit the elk situation to a group of ecologists for discussion.

By 1940, similar assertions were being made about a need to drastically reduce elk at Rocky Mountain National Park. Wildlife biologist Harold Ratcliff reported that elk were destroying the park and that they had consumed 90 percent of the willows along Beaver Meadows. Ratcliff argued strongly for a major reduction in animals. Not everyone agreed with the assessment that elk were degrading the park and its plant communities. There was significant opposition to any elk reduction, both by park staff and the public. A decline in beaver numbers was also being blamed on elk and deer, with some biologists arguing that heavy browsing of willow and aspen was negatively affecting beaver populations in the park.

As a result of these and other arguments, the Park Service decided to take drastic action. In January 1944, Rocky Mountain National Park was given authority to reduce its elk herd by any means necessary. The easiest means was shooting, and park rangers were given the task of eliminating elk that not many decades earlier they had worked hard to protect. Through the shooting program, park elk numbers were reduced from an estimated 1,525 to an average of 587 for the years between 1949 and 1961. By 1962, elk populations were reduced to 350 animals.

The effect of this reduction on other wildlife was barely considered. For example, some animals, such as bears, foxes, ravens, wolverines, and magpies depend on winter-killed wildlife carrion for their survival. Elk reductions surely reduced the food available to these scavengers and may even have led to the extinction of the wolverine.

Finally, in 1964, a cooperative research report among the Forest Service, National Park Service, and Colorado Division of Wildlife stated that the development on historic winter range in the Estes Park area not only reduced available habitat for wintering elk, but also blocked migration corridors to lower-elevation foothills. It also noted that though elk numbers were limited by declining range conditions, the park's elk herds were among the most prolific in Colorado, suggesting that perhaps range conditions were not as bad as reported. Fertility and survival of elk calves are significantly related to availability of nutrients and the degree of wintertime stress. The report concluded that the available winter range could support only 400 to 600 animals. Hunting and trapping removed animals that were considered excess.

In 1968, the Park Service embarked on a new policy of natural regulation. Under this policy, animals would be permitted to fluctuate according to the influence of food availability and quality, climatic conditions, disease, and predation. Those who thought Rocky Mountain National Park was already overpopulated with elk disagreed vehemently with this policy.

Without intrusive management, the population of elk continued to grow larger, and by 1998, summertime park populations of elk were estimated at 3,200 to 3,700 animals, of which 25 to 30 percent wintered in the park, while the rest migrated to lands beyond park borders. This is a far greater number of animals than biologists had estimated could be supported, given the availability of forage, suggesting that earlier estimates of carrying capacity may have been too conservative.

The issue of overgrazing is complex. One problem with earlier assumptions that elk were overgrazing the park is the presumption that elk browsing has the same effect as the grazing of domestic livestock. There are, however, substantial differences between the way domestic livestock use the landscape and the way native herbivore species influence plant communities.

When plants are cropped is critical to their survival. If browsed or grazed repeatedly during the summer growing season, year after year, as occurs with domestic livestock, plants can be weakened to the point where they can be effectively extirpated from the landscape. Native herbivores, however, are much more widely dispersed across the landscape than are domestic animals. In summer, elk are dispersed over so much of the landscape that no individual plant is likely to be grazed or browsed more than once in any single season. In Yellowstone National Park, for example, where elk are even more abundant than in Rocky Mountain National Park, research has demonstrated that grasshoppers consume 90 percent more of the aboveground biomass than do large ungulates such as elk.

Most of the heavy browsing and grazing by elk and deer occurs in winter, when these animals are concentrated by snow on a limited amount of available winter range. During the winter, plants are dormant, with most of their food resources stored in underground roots. Animal herbivory during the winter has far fewer negative effects upon plants than does summertime use. Plants are more tolerant of heavy browsing or cropping in winter. Aspens and willows, the species of most concern to critics of park policies, are able to grow from root suckers. So long as the plant isn't browsed in summer, it can survive severe winter browsing pressure.

Furthermore, populations of native herbivores, whether elk, moose, or deer, vary from year to year in response to harsh weather, disease, and other factors. This creates occasional respite from browsing and grazing pressure. Domestic livestock numbers, on the other hand, tend to remain constant, even in periods of drought and at other times when plant production has declined; thus the potential to do serious ecological damage is heightened.

Some biologists also question the interpretation of elk and deer browsing as negative. They argue that elk and deer "predation" upon browse species is no different from wolf predation upon elk or deer, or how fires change the makeup of tree species in a forest. Why shouldn't we expect elk or deer have an influence upon willow or aspen?

Blaming all aspen decline on ungulates such as elk and deer, say park policy supporters, may be simplistic. Aspen is also heavily dependent upon fire to stimulate sucker production. Many of the aspen groves in Rocky Mountain National Park expanded late in the last century due to fires, both those caused by lightning and those ignited by humans. Fire suppression has probably disrupted some natural cycles and allowed forests to invade aspen sites.

Another variable that critics of park policies have failed to consider, say supporters of the natural regulation policy, is changing climatic conditions. Aspen and willow are both dependent upon high soil moisture. Many of the stands of aspen and willow expanded during the Little Ice Age, which ended around 1850. This was a period of higher-than-average moisture. Since the mid-1800s, there has been a gradual drying of the climate throughout the West, resulting in stress and decline in some moisture-dependent species. Between 1907 and 1998, there was an average annual decline in precipitation of a half inch and an increase in temperature of almost a degree. Such small differences may not seem like much, but Rocky Mountain National Park is a relatively dry, arid environ-

Aspen in Horseshoe Park, with dark scar tissue where elk have browsed on the bark in winter. Development of scar tissue is a defense mechanism to discourage future browsing by elk and other animals.

ment, and even a change of a half inch in annual moisture could be significant.

What's important isn't any precise measure of animals, park policy supporters suggest, but that ecological processes are permitted to operate freely. This includes allowing herds to fluctuate in response to forage quality, climatic conditions, and other factors without significant human intervention. Much of the debate centers on how one interprets the evidence and how it is viewed. Critics point to the declining vigor and number of willows and aspen trees and claim that elk and deer populations need to be reduced, while others see the same processes and suggest that willow and aspen are early successional species that are doomed to be replaced on a site anyway. Most of the elk and deer herds in the West are manipulated by hunting, and parks such as Rocky Mountain can provide a place where nature, not humans, influences elk and deer herds.

Reaching a consensus on ungulate management is no closer today than sixty years ago. But how the controversy is resolved may shape not only plant communities, but also the entire management philosophy of the parks.

Future controversies include discussion about limiting or restricting use in the park. Some park advocates claim that the influx of too many people is spoiling the park's natural resources and degrading the park experience for visitors. To deal with growing numbers of visitors, the Park Service has already instituted some modifications to earlier policies. For example, a shuttle bus now carries visitors to the Bear Lake Parking Lot to reduce congestion on the road, and there is talk of shuttle buses for the Trail Ridge Road.

Development in and around the park continues to reduce big-game winter range, as well as the opportunities for allowing fires to burn, and air pollution from the cities on the plains sometimes obscures skies. Rocky Mountain National Park is becoming an island in a sea of human development. Conservation biologists have noted that small preserves such as Rocky Mountain National Park are not sufficiently large enough to protect and preserve ecological processes and support viable populations of most species. Unless surrounding national forest lands are managed primarily for natural processes as well, Rocky Mountain National Park will likely end up biologically impoverished. In recognition of this need for large ecological reserves, there has been a change in management policies on other public lands to make all fit together as a larger whole.

Development outside of the park in Estes Park and surrounding valleys threatens to isolate wildlife populations in the park, eliminating migration corridors and ultimately reducing the opportunities for wildland restoration.

Finally, there is some support for restoring wolves to the park and surrounding national forest lands. No doubt this will also generate some heated discussion and opposition. Rocky Mountain National Park was born in controversy and will likely continue to be the center of controversy as society tries to determine exactly what kind of park it wants in the twenty-first century.

PLANTS

Due to its overall high elevation and harsh climatic conditions, the plant communities in Rocky Mountain National Park are not as diverse as those in some other national parks. Nevertheless, the park does provide a good representation of the major plant species found in the southern Rocky Mountains. In total, there are approximately 900 species of plants.

Plant distribution and occurrence are affected by many factors, including soils, moisture, temperature, aspect, past disturbance, and elevation. Elevation and disturbance such as wildfire or avalanche have the greatest overriding influences upon plant distribution. In general, the higher in elevation, the colder, the shorter the growing season, and the greater the moisture, in the form of snow. Many things influence this general statement, however. Wind can blow away snow from many alpine areas, creating virtual deserts, even though annual precipitation might be significant.

Within Rocky Mountain National Park, there are three major vegetation zones: montane, subalpine, and alpine tundra. There are also a few more localized plant communities associated with specialized habitat, such as the riparian vegetation found along streams and wetlands and the mountain grasslands, or parks, as they are called in the Rockies.

Elevations in Rocky Mountain National Park span nearly 7,000 feet, from 7,640 feet at the lowest parts of the park to the summit of 14,256-foot Longs Peak. With over one-third of the park's area above 11,000 feet, Rocky Mountain supports one of the most extensive areas of alpine tundra of any park in the country.

Montane Zone

The montane zone occupies the lowest elevations, between 7,600 and 9,000 feet. On the sunniest, warmest sites, the cinnamon-barked ponderosa pine forms relatively open savannas, with a well-developed under-

Loco weed and aspen in Moraine Valley.

story of mountain muhly grass and shrubs like antelope bitterbrush. On cooler, north-facing slopes is found Douglas fir, often intermixed with ponderosa pine, and at higher elevations, sometimes lodgepole pine.

There are some subtle but notable differences in vegetation between the eastern and western sides of the park. The eastern region receives less precipitation, with Estes Park recording about 13 inches of moisture a year

(Tucson, Arizona, by comparison, gets 12 inches). The low precipitation is exacerbated by the frequent, drying chinook winds, which absorb moisture, drying out soils more rapidly than usual. Grand Lake, on the west slope, receives 19 to 20 inches or more of precipitation in a typical year. The larger amount of moisture on the west slope results in greater weathering of rock and deeper, moister soils. The abundance of moisture affects plant distribution and species composition. On the west slope, vegetation

Ponderosa pine has needles in groups of three and a reddish, flaky bark.

Natural meadows, such as these in Horseshoe Park, are dominated by needle and thread grass, mountain muhly, June grass, and blue grama.

is more continuous and luxuriant. Sagebrush tends to dominate the drier south-facing slopes, while moister sites are typically forests with lodgepole pine rather than the ponderosa pine so common on the eastern slope.

Natural meadow communities or parks found in this zone are dominated by needle and thread grass, mountain muhly, June grass, and blue grama, plus numerous flowering forbs in early spring to summer. Other common meadow grass species include hairgrass, redtop, and reflexed bluegrass. In some areas, big sagebrush is also common. In formerly cultivated areas, you may find timothy, smooth brome, or Kentucky bluegrass.

Ecological Adaptations in the Montane Zone

Ponderosa pine is the most distinctive species in the montane zone. With its broad, open crown, reddish bark, and long needles, it's one of the easiest trees to identify in Rocky Mountain National Park. Living as it does on arid, warm sites at the lower limits for tree growth, the success of ponderosa pine is due to several adaptations. First, the tree develops a long taproot early in life to gather moisture from a wide area. A three-inch seedling may have a root more than two feet long. Mature ponderosa pines possess lateral roots up to 100 feet long.

While this root system helps ponderosa pine survive the often droughty conditions it experiences in its preferred habitat, successfully establishing on a site is a difficult process. Ponderosa pine, like most conifers, only produces good seed crops every three to five years. But an abundance of seeds is not the only requirement for successful reproduction; there also has to be sufficient soil moisture in the spring and early summer for seedlings to establish themselves. Abundant seed and high soil moisture occur simultaneously only once every forty to sixty years. But in a long-lived species like ponderosa pine, which may attain ages of 500 to 600 years, infrequent successful reproduction is not a problem.

Ponderosa pine seeds germinate best where there are open, sunny conditions. In most of the West, as well as in Rocky Mountain National Park, this is promoted by periodic wildfire. Historically, lightning, and sometimes even humans, ignited low-intensity blazes that occurred every five to thirty years. Such fires swept through a forest, consuming pine needles, grass, and small shrubs, but rarely killing the old-growth trees. Indeed, prior to widespread fire suppression and the advent of livestock grazing, which removed the fine grass and other litter that carried the blazes, wildfire maintained many ponderosa pine stands throughout the West in an open, parklike condition. While fires killed the younger pine seedlings, the older trees usually survived because their thick bark protected them from all but the hottest blazes.

Douglas fir is another easy tree to identify. It has soft needles and three-pronged scales on its cones that look something like the hind legs and tail of a mouse. With its thick, corky bark and Christmas tree–like shape, Douglas fir is an attractive species. It occurs on moist, shady northern slopes of the montane zone at lower elevations but gradually shifts to the south-facing slopes above 9,000 feet. The tree seldom forms pure stands but tends to be mixed among other forest species. Like ponderosa pine, older Douglas firs have very thick bark and are not damaged by smaller fires. Nevertheless, like the pine, Douglas fir germinates best on open, sunny, bare mineral soil—the kinds of conditions created by fire. If fires fail to thin the Douglas fir forests, disease and insects do the job. In recent years, many of the Douglas fir forests in Rocky Mountain National Park have been attacked by spruce budworm, killing some of the trees. The insects, however, provide tremendous food resources for many warblers, nuthatches, and other insect-eating birds.

Aspen is another important tree of the montane zone. Although it is a prodigious producer of seeds, the seeds have high moisture requirements, and most fail to successfully establish themselves. Indeed, there is no evidence that aspen have reproduced from seeds in the Rockies since the close of the last ice age, except in Yellowstone, where the big fires of 1988 created unusual conditions for aspen seed establishment. Most aspen trees regenerate by sending up suckers or new stems from their roots. Damage or destruction to aboveground boles, or trunks, stimulates the production of root suckers, and as a consequence, most aspen stands are perpetuated by periodic disturbance such as fire, insects, or browsing by large herbivores such as elk and moose.

Wildfires are probably responsible for most aspen stand establishment. Unlike pine, whose thick bark enables it to survive fires, aspen has thin bark, and the aboveground boles are easily killed by fire. But fire doesn't usually kill the aspen tree's roots, which are protected by the overlying soil. If the aboveground boles are destroyed, the aspen puts out suckers or new boles from the large root system. Because many aspen groves are connected by a massive root system, they are often made up of genetically identical clones. This is very obvious in the autumn, when the hillside aspen stands begin to change colors. Each clone will change color at a slightly different rate than adjacent clones, and the color of the leaves will vary somewhat as well. So you might find a group of trees that is all golden while an adjacent stand is still green.

Aspen trees are also adapted to periodic heavy browsing from ungulates such as elk and moose. Elk, in particular, forage on aspen branches and bark in winter, when other foods such as grasses or shrubs are covered by deep snows. Many of the older aspens in Rocky Mountain National Park have dark, thick, corky bark on their lower boles. This is scar tissue, which develops after elk or other animals chew off a part of the outer bark. But with aspen, as with grass, what happens to the aboveground boles is far less important than maintaining the roots. So long as the trees can photosynthesize in summer, they can maintain their root system. Fortunately, nearly all of the browsing on aspen occurs in winter, when the trees are dormant. This has little long-term impact on the tree, since aspen is able to produce leaves in summer, restoring its store of nutrients to the roots.

Aspen and ponderosa pine along Cub Lake Trail. These trees are both adapted to periodic fire, which helps rejuvenate stands.

Lodgepole pine tends to grow in dense thickets that establish after wildfires burn through the area.

Lodgepole pine also common in the montane forests, particularly on the west slope of the park in the Kawuneeche Valley along the North Fork of the Colorado and adjacent tributaries. Lodgepole pine is also dependent on periodic disturbance to maintain its dominant position in the forest landscape. Unlike ponderosa pine, lodgepole pine grows at higher elevations where snow is deeper. Here, fires are less frequent than at lower elevations. When they do occur, they tend to be hot stand replacement blazes (meaning that the entire stand of trees is killed and replaced by new trees). But a big fire is a welcome event to a lodgepole forest. The lodgepole has serotinous cones, which are covered with a resinous bond that prevents the scales from opening and shedding seeds until they are heated. Serotiny is genetically controlled and varies among individuals and populations. Not all lodgepole cones have the same degree of serotiny, and some will open even in the absence of fire. Nevertheless, remaining closed until a fire is an ecological adaptation that contributes to the dominance of lodgepole pine upon a site, ensuring a good seeding after a blaze. After one fire in Colorado, researchers found more than 44,000 trees per acre twenty-two years after the blaze. Such dense thickets are called "doghair" stands.

Once lodgepole pine reseeds an area, it grows rapidly. Indeed, it can produce viable cones in five to ten years, whereas other conifers may require fifty to seventy-five years to produce viable cones. This enables the pine to colonize the area rapidly, beating out the competition for growing sites. As a consequence of their common origins after a blaze, most lodgepole stands tend to have a uniform age, size, and height. After 250 to 300 years, the stands break up as a result of insects, blowdown, and disease. In the small openings created, younger pine trees may become established.

Subalpine Zone

The subalpine zone runs from 9,000 to 11,000 feet and has the most luxuriant vegetation in the park. It could well be called the snow forest, for it receives the heaviest snowfall of any zone in the park, often reaching depths of five feet or more on the ground. Due to the heavy forest cover, snow melts slowly, ensuring adequate soil moisture for plant growth well into the summer. This is largely a forested zone dominated by Engelmann spruce and subalpine fir. Spruce and fir both possess narrow crowns, with the fir having downward spraying branches that tend to shed snow. Understory cover is commonly red huckleberry, myrtle blueberry, star-flowered pyrola, heartleaf arnica, chiming bells, groundsel, blue columbine, prince's pine, and Jacob's ladder.

At the transition between the montane and subalpine zones, aspen and lodgepole pine are common in burned areas, often forming pure stands. On rocky, windswept ridges grow the picturesque twisted trunks of limber pine.

At the highest elevations, Engelmann spruce, subalpine fir, and limber pine all assume a stunted, twisted krummholz growth pattern, which is German for "crooked trunk." Both spruce and fir will form wind shear "fences," where the tree in front provides protection for the tree behind, and snow often covers the branches, allowing a gradual increase in the height of each succeeding tree. If heavy snow pushes a lower branch to the ground and pins it there, the branch will sometimes take root, establishing a new root system. Vegetative reproduction dominates at higher elevations, where harsh climatic conditions are unfavorable for seedling establishment. Despite such conditions, old-growth stands of spruce sometimes reach 400 to 500 years of age, and individuals may be 3 feet or more in girth. Spruce and fir are able to persist, and even grow to large size, here because they are able to photosynthesize at lower temperatures than other conifers. This substantially lengthens the season of growth.

Spruce and fir tend to be self-perpetuating. Unlike the ponderosa pine, lodgepole pine, and Douglas fir of the montane zone, spruce and fir can both successfully regenerate in the deep shade common in these forests. Of the two, spruce seedlings are more tolerant of sun and are often the ones to recolonize burned areas and other openings at higher elevations.

Limber pine becomes common above 9,000 feet on rocky ridges and shallow soil sites. Hikers on the trail to Dream Lake will pass through a group of limber pine in the midst of a spruce-fir forest. Here the pine have colonized a rocky ridge. Limber pine often takes on a stunted krummholz form in windy areas and near timberline, growing very picturesque, wind-twisted branches and trunks. The weight of snow is not usually a problem for limber pine, whose flexible branches bend under heavy snow, dumping the load. Plus, given its preferred habitat on windy ridges, the limber pine's branches are often blown free of snow.

Meadow areas in the subalpine tend to be dominated by tufted hairgrass, sheep fescue, and Parry's clover.

Engelmann spruce. This tree and subalpine fir are the primary species in the spruce-fir zone.

Spruce along the North Fork Colorado River. The spruce-fir belt is the zone of greatest snowfall. The narrow crown of subalpine fir and Engelmann spruce sheds snow and is an adaptation to their environment.

Alpine Tundra Zone

Tundra is a Russian term meaning "land of no trees." Originally referring to land in the Arctic, the term has come to mean any large expanse of above-timberland landscape. In the Rockies, the term alpine refers to the location of the tundra on mountaintops.

Alpine tundra is found on all mountain summits in Rocky Mountain National Park that reach above timberline, roughly 11,000 to 11,500 feet. The park probably has the most accessible and extensive example of alpine tundra found in the West, and it's certainly one of the features of greatest interest to visitors. The Trail Ridge Road provides easy access to this zone, and many of the trails in the park climb into the alpine region as well.

Hikers on the alpine tundra of Mount Chapin in the Mummy Range.

Approximately half of the alpine species found in Rocky Mountain National Park are identical to species found in the Arctic. The Southern Rockies, which includes Rocky Mountain National Park, has a well-developed alpine tundra zone for a variety of reasons. One is the abundance of north-south-oriented mountain ranges, which have provided an ideal migration corridor for arctic-alpine flora. In addition, due to the overall aridity of the Southern Rockies, there was a comparatively large amount of unglaciated high-elevation terrain that created a refuge for arctic-alpine species. A short growing season, severe wind, high-intensity solar radiation, and not infrequently, drought as a result of drying winds dominate alpine areas.

Major Alpine Plant Communities

Within the broad zone known as alpine tundra, there are distinct plant associations. Four major ones are found in Rocky Mountain National Park: turf, meadow, snowfield, and fellfield (rock garden) communities.

Grasses and sedges dominate turf communities, which are typically found in areas where wind tends to blow away the snow in winter. As a consequence, such areas are relatively dry. Without snow to protect plant leaves in winter, wind abrasion is a major problem for plants living here. Plants common in alpine turf areas include *Kobresia myosuroides*, along with alpine harebell, alpine forget-me-not, alpine primrose, and yellow paintbrush. Elk heavily graze the nutritious *Kobresia* in the summer, giving rise to the common name elk sedge.

Alpine meadow communities contain a profusion of flowers in summer. These sites tend to have deeper soils and greater moisture than the turf communities. They typically are found in shallow, well-drained swales where snow may collect, providing some protection from harsh winds, but they become snow-free relatively quickly in early summer. Common flowers of the meadow community include mountain avens, American bistort, mountain harebell, alpine chiming bell, and sky pilot.

Snowfield communities differ from other alpine sites in that a heavy snow cover accumulates in winter and often doesn't melt until midsummer or later, resulting in an even shorter growing season and typically cold, saturated soils. Snowfield communities occur in the lee of boulders, ridges, and other areas where windblown snow accumulates in winter. A number of sedges are common in these communities, including Drummond's rush and Pyrenean sedge, along with grasses such as alpine timothy and tufted hairgrass. Flowers include snow buttercup, alpine avens, and Parry clover. If the site stays saturated for most of the growing season, you may find marsh marigold, elephanthead, globeflower, and star gentian.

Fellfield communities are found on rocky sites. Soils tend to be coarse textured, and wind frequently removes winter snow cover, exposing plants to the full blast of gales. Fellfield communities are dominated by mat-forming and cushionlike plants such as phlox, rock jasmine, and mountain avens.

Ecological Adaptations of Alpine Plants

Alpine plants display a number of adaptations to their harsh environment. The plants of this zone tend to be long-lived perennials. There are few annuals here; these are precluded by the short growing season, which limits seed set. There are also a significant number of sedges, grasses, lichens, and mosses, all of which are quite hardy and enter dormancy whenever conditions are not suitable for growth.

Perhaps the most memorable feature of alpine regions for most people is the dwarf plants that dot the tundra with colorful blossoms of magenta, yellow, blue, purple, rose, and white throughout the short alpine summer. The leaves and stalks tend to be smaller and the number of flowers on each plant fewer than on similar low-elevation species. Their small size keeps the plants closer to the ground, where microsite temperatures are often warmer, and also provides protection from the wind. Despite the small stems and leaves, the flower blossoms are frequently quite large. Several factors are responsible for this. Larger blossoms gather more solar radiation than smaller blossoms, helping to heat up the plants' physiological processes, and they also attract more pollinating insects.

Another adaptation to cold is the presence of anthocyanin, a red pigment that gives alpine plants darker coloration. This helps the plants absorb heat and is important for cold-hardiness. Because of their adaptations to cold, alpine plants can begin to photosynthesize when temperatures are just above freezing.

Mountain Riparian Areas

Riparian areas are the thin, green lines of lush, water-dependent vegetative growth found along streams, seeps, and lakes. Riparian vegetation is usually not limited by precipitation. Such plant communities are rather lush, given the overall arid climate of Colorado.

Riparian zone along Hidden Valley Creek. Riparian areas are critical habitat for 70 to 80 percent of the West's wildlife, providing shelter, food, and water.

In Rocky Mountain National Park, the dominant tree species found in riparian communities include narrowleaf cottonwood, balsam poplar, and an occasional blue spruce, which reaches its upper limits around 9,000 feet. Shrubs include dwarf birch, river birch, willows, chokecherry, red osier dogwood, alder, and Rocky Mountain maple. Most of these species produce an abundance of seeds that readily colonize bare soils and gravel bars.

The lower end of Wild Basin contains one of the few undisturbed willow carr (similar to a bog, but basic rather than acidic) communities in Colorado. Willows and sedges dominate this wetland, through which runs the North St. Vrain River.

Fire Ecology

Fire scars on 50-million-year-old petrified trees in Yellowstone National Park demonstrate that wildfires have always been a major ecological force in many forest and grassland ecosystems. The scenery of Rocky Mountain National Park is a direct consequence of wildfire. Most of the forested areas of the park have burned at one time or another. So if you find pleasure in the golden glow of aspen and the open ponderosa forests, you're experiencing the aftermath of wildfire. Evidence of past fires abounds in the park. Much of the upper North Fork of the Colorado drainage burned in the 1860s, the area around Jackstraw Mountain burned in 1871, and the area along Glacier Creek and Glacier Basin Campground burned in 1900. The most recent fire, the Ouzel blaze, burned about 1,000 acres in 1978.

Since the 1920s, Rocky Mountain National Park and surrounding national forests have attempted to put out nearly all blazes, with varying degrees of success. In the past, many of the fires that burned through what is now Rocky Mountain National Park likely started outside the park, particularly at the drier lower elevations. These fires often burned upslope and into the higher elevations of the Front Range.

Evidence suggests that fire suppression has reduced the frequency of fires, at least at lower elevations, and as a consequence may have reduced the number of fires occurring upslope in the park. Nevertheless, humans can never completely eliminate fire from the landscape. The only thing we can successfully do is change the timing of blazes. And under certain conditions of high winds and drought, no human efforts can stop a fire. Most fires go out not because firefighters put them out, but because the weather changed. You'll often hear the media report that firefighters got the blaze under control, but this is typically because it rained or snowed. In fact, research has shown that most fires go out on their own without any suppression and seldom burn more than a few acres. However, under the right conditions of wind, drought, and fuels, the largest blazes raze hundreds of thousands of acres. Yet these conditions occur so infrequently that large blazes tend to occur only once every 100 or 200 years.

Fire scar on ponderosa pine. Fire frequency varied throughout the different ecological zones of the park. The lower-elevation ponderosa pine forests burned frequently; the higher elevation spruce-fir forest had fewer fires, often hundreds of years apart.

The ponderosa pine forests in Rocky Mountain National Park had a mean fire interval of 31 to 37 years. Historically, the time between blazes ranged between 4 and 116 years. In lodgepole pine stands, the mean fire interval was 51 years. In the snowy subalpine forest zone, the interval between fires was 100 to 300 years. Given the long intervals between blazes in this zone, fire suppression has probably had a minimal effect on stand composition.

Fires do not burn on some precise clocklike schedule, however. It's simplistic to generalize and suggest that all fires that occurred in these ponderosa forest stands were low-intensity burns. There were times, particularly during periodic wetter climatic periods, when blazes were less frequent and decades could go by without a fire. During these long intervals, fuels built up and the density of trees increased—not unlike the situation today as a consequence of fire suppression. When a fire finally did occur, it often burned hotter and leaped into the crowns or tops of trees, burning far more acres and killing not only small trees, but also some of the larger trees in the process.

Nevertheless, most blazes, even larger fires, seldom kill all the trees. The flames leap and dance across the landscape in a mosaic pattern, leaving patches of unburnt forest. After the passage of the fire, these remaining trees provide the seeds to begin a new forest. As a result of such blazes, fuels are reduced, ensuring that no similar large blazes occur for decades.

Unfortunately, like the cultural bias society once had against predators such as wolves, we don't yet appreciate the numerous benefits of wildfires. We say the blazes destroyed or devastated so many acres of forest. Yet fires are one of the major evolutionary forces that shape the majority of plant communities in the West. Fires, even big fires, don't devastate forests; rather, they are a rejuvenating force that thins the forests, recycles nutrients, and may even help create soil when intense heat cracks boulders and rocks.

Understory of subalpine fir growing up among mature lodgepole pine. If ignited, the highly flammable subalpine fir helps blazes burn up into the crowns of trees to create a stand replacement canopy burn.

If fires are suppressed, or simply fail to burn an area for a significant period of time, other factors begin to compensate for the lack of fire-caused mortality. Another natural thinning agent in forest stands is insects. Pine beetles, for example, will attack dense stands of trees, boring into the bark and laying their eggs. The beetle larvae consume the inner cambium layer of the tree, often killing the host tree. But pine beetles are not likely to kill an entire forest. Once a sufficient number of trees have died, the remaining trees, with more water and nutrients available to them, are usually able to repel the beetles.

The resulting dead trees, known as snags, whether due to fires, insects, or disease, are critical to the forest ecosystem. Ecologically speaking, dead trees are not a wasted resource. Indeed, they are essential to the long-term viability of the forest. Snags provide nesting sites for many cavity-nesting birds, including woodpeckers, bluebirds, and even some ducks. Bats, squirrels, and martens all use snags as well. If a snag falls to the ground, it provides a home for many insects, including ants, as well as hiding cover for small mammals such as voles. If the snag happens to fall into a river or stream, it helps to stabilize the bank against erosion and provides cover for fish like trout. In fact, it could be argued that dead trees are as critical to the continued life of the forest ecosystem as live trees.

Fires need to be restored to Rocky Mountain National Park. And it's not just small blazes that must be restored, but the occasional large stand replacement blaze as well. Fires that burn tens of thousands of acres at a time are not unusual from an historical perspective.

Rather than suppress wildfires, a more strategic response would be for agencies to fireproof nearby communities like Estes Park. Firebreaks can be constructed around such communities for far less than it costs to fight one major blaze.

Species Accounts

The following species accounts cover all the major tree species in Rocky Mountain National Park, plus some of the more common shrubs and flowers. This is not a complete listing of all 900 plant species.

Exercise caution when interpreting species descriptions; recognize that great variability exists in nature. All colors, sizes, and other descriptive information are only approximate to give a general idea of the size of the plant, key feature, or its color patterns.

Trees

SUBALPINE FIR
(Abies lasiocarpa)

Description. Very narrow crown, somewhat spikelike. Height to 80 feet. Branches on trunk to the ground. Needles about 1 inch long, dense on branch, and soft to touch (spruce needles are stiff and pointed). Needles twirl upward on twig. Bark thin, smooth, gray with small horizontal ridges and resin blisters. In older trees, bottom part of the trunk bark becomes more furrowed. Purple cones grow upright from branches (unlike most conifers, whose cones hang down) and are clustered at the top of the tree. Cones turn brown at maturity and disintegrate on the branch, which is why you seldom find intact fir cones on the ground.

Distribution. Subalpine forests from 9,500 to 11,500 feet. One of the most widely distributed conifers in North America, found from the Yukon to New Mexico. Common throughout Rocky Mountain National Park in the subalpine zone.

Remarks. Near timberline, where conditions for successful seed establishment are difficult, subalpine fir will often reproduce by layering, with lower branches pressed to the ground by snow, producing roots and a new tree.

Engelmann spruce can be distinguished by the cones clustered near the top of the tree and hanging down.

ENGELMANN SPRUCE
(Picea engelmannii)

Description. Tall, straight trunk with conical crown; branches cover trunk nearly to the ground. Height to 100 feet. Dark green needles are 1 inch long and four-sided, and can be rounded between the fingers. Feels sharp to touch. Soft hairs cover branchlets. Bark has thin, platelike scales; generally gray but sometimes reddish. Tan cones 1 to 2 inches, with papery scales. Cones hang down from branches, generally on upper third of tree.

Distribution. Spruce is the dominant tree in the subalpine forest. Grows on moist, deep soils from 9,500 to 11,500 feet. Often forms timberline islands of stunted krummholz trees.

Remarks. Spruce may live 500 years or more.

BLUE SPRUCE
(Picea pungens)

Description. Conical with branches on trunk nearly to ground. Needles four-sided and sharp to touch. Smooth branchlets, rather than hairy as in Englemann spruce. Bark furrowed and usually brown. Cone scales thin and papery, with wavy margin. Dusky blue color of foliage varies from tree to tree; may be green.
Distribution. Along streams up to 9,000 feet, often growing in small clumps or as individual trees. Not very common in Rocky Mountain National Park.
Remarks. Blue spruce will sometimes hybridize with Englemann spruce, making ID more difficult. Such trees are more green than blue. Long-lived tree, often up to 800 years old.

Colorado blue spruce is typically found at lower elevations along rivers and streams.

LODGEPOLE PINE
(Pinus contorta)

Description. Tall, straight, slender trunk with little taper (lodgepole pines are often used for telephone poles). In dense stands, lower branches self-prune. Needles 1 to 2 inches, in groups of two. Cone oval and 2 inches in diameter, growing at the tips of branches. Bark thin and brownish, though sometimes reddish where exposed to the sun.

Distribution. One of the most widely distributed trees in the West. Found from Alaska to southern California, and throughout the Rockies from Colorado northward. Lodgepole pine colonizes areas burned by fires and is very common in the upper montane and lower sub-alpine zone of Rocky Mountain National Park between 8,500 and 10,500 feet. More common west of the Divide, and one of the most common trees in the North Fork of the Colorado drainage.

Remarks. Named for its straight, slender boles, which Plains Indians used for tepee poles in their "lodges." Interestingly, its Latin name *contorta* refers to a twisted, stunted variety of lodgepole pine that grows along the coast of the Pacific Northwest. The species was first described in this location, hence its Latin name.

LIMBER PINE
(Pinus flexilis)

Description. Open, rounded crown with multiple branches. Needles 2 inches, in clusters of five per bundle. Bark dark gray. Extremely flexible branches. Cylindrical cones 4 to 5 inches long.

Distribution. Found on rocky areas, primarily windswept ridges at higher elevations up to 11,500 feet. Limber pines are one of the first species to grow in burn areas too high in elevation for lodgepole pines and aspen.

Remarks. Limber pine possess very long taproots, allowing them to survive on dry, rocky ridges. The large seeds are a favorite food of the Clark's nutcracker.

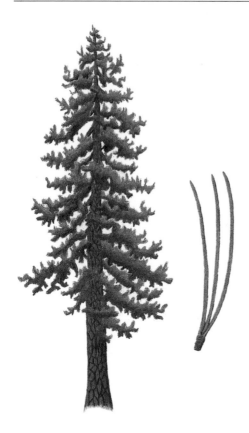

PONDEROSA PINE
(Pinus ponderosa)

Description. Open, rounded crown, with flat-topped crowns common in the oldest individuals. Lower trunk on mature trees typically branch-free due to self-pruning. Needles long, up to 7 inches, in clusters of three needles per bundle. Bark reddish brown in plates that can be flicked off easily. Globe-shaped cones 3 to 5 inches in length, with spines at tips of scales. **Distribution.** Very wide distribution throughout the West. There are three varieties of ponderosa pine in the West, with the variety found in Rocky Mountain National Park—*Pinus ponderosa* var. *scopulorum*—the smallest of the three. In the park, ponderosa pine forms open woodlands in the montane zone east of the divide up to 9,000 feet in elevation. Very rare west of the Divide, although an occasional individual can be found near Inlet by Grand Lake. **Remarks.** Ponderosa pine is readily adapted to surviving fires. The self-pruning of its lower branches helps eliminate the possibility of flames leaping up into the crown, plus the bark is thick and readily repels small blazes. As the bark heats up, the platelike scales pop off before they ignite, and by this mechanism, the pine avoids serious damage from all but the most intense blazes.

DOUGLAS FIR
(*Pseudotsuga menziesii*)

Description. Open, broad crown with self-pruning of lower branches in older individuals. Needles 1 to 2 inches, flat, stalked, round-tipped, and soft to touch. Not a true fir, with cones hanging down instead of upright as on true firs. Cones brownish and 3 inches long, with a three-part bract that sticks out from scales. Bark grayish brown and very thick in mature specimens.

Distribution. Douglas fir is widespread throughout the West but reaches its greatest size in the Pacific Northwest. The variety found in Rocky Mountain National Park is smaller and adapted to the more arid conditions of the Rockies. In the park, Douglas fir typically grows in the montane zone between ponderosa pine and the subalpine spruce-fir forests at elevations of 8,500 to 9,500 feet. At the lower elevations, it's typically found on cooler, north-facing slopes, but as it climbs in elevation, it shifts to the warmer, south-facing slopes.

Remarks. Named for David Douglas, a Scottish botanist who first described the tree in Oregon. Douglas fir often survives low-intensity blazes because its thick bark and self-pruning habit offer protection from fires.

COMMON JUNIPER
(*Juniperus communis* var. *alpina*)

Description. Low-growing, prostrate shrub. Sharp needles. Seed a bluish "berry."
Distribution. Found circumpolar. In Rocky Mountain National Park, open, dry slopes from low elevations to alpine.
Remarks. Juniper "berries" are an important food for birds and mammals.

ROCKY MOUNTAIN JUNIPER
(*Juniperus scopulorum*)

Description. Open-crowned, much-branched shrub or small tree up to 25 feet tall. Needles scalelike, overlapping one another like shingles. Cones are small, bluish "berries." Bark grayish.
Distribution. Lowest, driest, rockiest elevations of Rocky Mountain National Park, mixed in the ponderosa pine zone.
Remarks. Sometimes called western red cedar.

ASPEN
(*Populus tremuloides*)

Description. Smooth, white to light tan bark, although lower trunk may be dark gray with scar tissue where elk have browsed upon the bark. Broad, oval leaves with flattened stems; light green in summer and golden in autumn. Often grows in clumps or groves.

Distribution. Found on moist soils in all zones from montane to timberline, but most abundant below 10,000 feet, where it grows on the edges of meadows and along streams. Also invades burned areas. The only deciduous tree commonly seen growing outside of the riparian areas in the montane and subalpine zones. Particularly abundant in Horseshoe Park, Moraine Park, lower end of Wild Basin, and along the North Fork of the Colorado River Valley.

Remarks. Aspen grow genetically identical clones that are attached by roots. If the aboveground boles are killed, aspen sends up hundreds of new shoots, known as suckers. Genetically connected clones can often be detected in autumn when the leaves change, since each clone changes color at a slightly different time and rate. Aspen is a favorite food of beavers and elk.

NARROWLEAF COTTONWOOD
(*Populus angustifolia*)

Description. Narrow, lanceolate leaves up to 4 inches long. Bark smooth on young trees but becomes rough and furrowed on mature trees. Leaf buds have an aromatic smell in late spring. Leaves green in summer, turning golden in autumn. Downy white seeds look like cotton fibers and are released in spring.

Distribution. Along the margins of streams and wetlands up to 10,000 feet.

Remarks. Cottonwood is a favorite food of beavers.

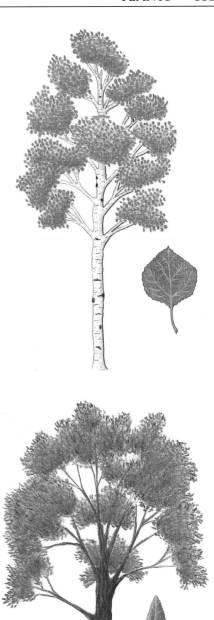

BALSAM POPLAR
(*Populus balsamifera*)

Description. Leaves dark green above and lighter below. Can be distinguished from narrowleaf cottonwood, which it resembles, by its ovate leaves. Bark smooth on young trees but becomes furrowed on lower trunks of older trees.
Distribution. Rare south of Canada but found in a few locations in Rocky Mountain National Park, including lower part of Fern Lake Trail, Moraine Park, Horseshoe Park, and Wild Basin.
Remarks. The buds of this tree emit a very strong perfume in the spring that is distinctive to these forests.

Balsam poplar looks something like a cottonwood tree, but with slightly larger, wider leaves. It is uncommon in the park and in Colorado.

Shrubs

CHOKECHERRY
(Prunus virginiana)

Description. Up to 10 feet in height. Multibranched. Bark reddish brown. Leaves taper at both ends and possess finely serrated edges. Flowers fragrant, creamy white racemes, berries purple-red to black.
Distribution. Moist soil areas along streams and hillsides.
Remarks. The berries are a favorite food of birds and bears.

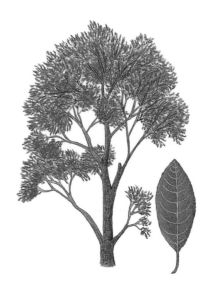

ROCKY MOUNTAIN THIMBLEBERRY
(Rubus deliciosus)

Description. Rounded, slightly three-lobed, bright green leaves. Bark light brown and shreddy. Large, white blossoms 1 to 3 inches across. Fruit raspberrylike and edible.
Distribution. East-slope areas with moist soil along streams.
Remarks. Sometimes called boulder raspberry.

ROCKY MOUNTAIN MAPLE
(Acer glabrum)

Description. Large shrub or small tree growing in multistem clumps. Gray bark. Twigs smooth and reddish in color. Leaves sharply toothed, palmate, with 3 to 5 lobes. Leaves turn yellow in autumn.
Distribution. Usually grows among rocks in montane and lower subalpine zones up to 10,000 feet.
Remarks. Elk and deer eat this shrub in winter.

RED OSIER DOGWOOD
(*Cornus stolonifera*)

Description. Multistemmed up to 6 feet. Dark red bark, ovate leaves opposite with pinnate veins. Small, white flowers borne in flat-topped clusters. White berries.
Distribution. Along streams in moist soils.
Remarks. Berries are important food for birds.

SHRUBBY CINQUEFOIL
(*Potentilla fruticosa*)

Description. Rounded shrub, usually no more than 3 feet high. Flowers yellow and roselike. Leaves have three to seven leaflets.
Distribution. Found in meadows from foothills to alpine.
Remarks. Common plant on the tundra from Rockies to Alaska.

Shrubby cinquefoil is common in the meadows throughout the park. It grows north all the way to Alaska's Brooks Range.

CLIFFBUSH
(Jamesia americana)

Description. Clusters of five-petaled, creamy white flowers. Opposite, ribbed leaves ovate with serrate edges. Velvet leaves turn reddish late in the growing season.
Distribution. On rocky ledges and in rock crevices in montane zone east of Continental Divide.
Remarks. Named for Dr. Edwin James, who accompanied the Stephen Long 1820 Rocky Mountain Expedition and collected the plant while climbing Pikes Peak. Longs Peak was discovered during this trip and named for the expedition leader.

SERVICEBERRY
(Amelanchier alnifolia)

Description. A multistemmed shrub with gray bark. Clusters of white flowers in spring and apple-shaped, blue-purple berries in late summer. Leaves round and toothed along edges from middle to tip.
Distribution. Along streams and on hillsides up to 9,000 feet.
Remarks. A second subspecies found in the park, *Amelanchier alnifolia* var. *pumila*, has smooth-edged leaves. The berries are edible, and birds and bears feast on them. Elk and deer browse on the shrubs in winter.

ANTELOPE BITTERBRUSH
(Purshia tridentata)

Description. Much-branched shrub. Numerous fragrant, yellow flowers in May and June. Leaves are 1 inch long, three-toothed, and wedge-shaped, looking something like a sagebrush leaf.
Distribution. Close to rocks in the ponderosa pine forest below 9,000 feet.
Remarks. An important browse species for deer, which heavily clip the shrub.

KINNIKINNICK
(*Arctostaphylos uva-ursi*)

Description. Evergreen, prostrate, trailing shrub, often forming mats no more than 6 inches tall. Glossy, thick, green leaves. Flowers waxy reddish pink-white and urn-shaped. Tiny red berries that look like cranberries in autumn, often persisting over winter.

Distribution. Dry soils throughout montane zone, often colonizing recently burned areas.

Remarks. Related to manzanita, an important element of the chaparral in California. The berries are eaten by many different wildlife species.

RUSSET BUFFALOBERRY
(*Shepherdia canadensis*)

Description. Low-growing shrub. Leaves opposite, ovate, dark green above and silver below. Flowers opposite. Rust-colored, hairy twigs. Pale yellow flowers appear before leaves. Orange-red berries in late summer.

Distribution. Shady woods in montane zone.

Remarks. Berries are bitter but are a favorite of bears.

MOUNTAIN WILLOW
(*Salix monticola*)

Description. Grows up to 15 feet. Crooked, yellow stems. In spring, has silver-white pussy willowlike catkins. Leaves lanceolate to oblong-lanceolate (narrow), with finely toothed edges and pointed tips.

Distribution. Most common tall willow in park in montane zone. Found along streams.

Remarks. More than thirty species of willows are found in Colorado, and distinguishing among species is sometimes difficult.

SCOULER WILLOW
(Salix scouleriana)

Description. Tall shrub or small tree. Pale yellow catkins, or "pussytoes," bloom before leaves are out. Oblanceolate leaves green above and pale beneath.
Distribution. Along streams up to 10,000 feet, but occasionally found on drier meadows. Seen at Bear Lake, Dream Lake, and along Trail Ridge Road.
Remarks. The only willow that may be found in Rocky Mountain National Park, growing in forests away from streamsides. Named for Dr. John Scouler, a companion of botanist David Douglas, for whom the Douglas fir is named.

Willows along the Big Thompson River. Scouler willow is one of the most common taller willows found along the park's streams.

NET-VEINED WILLOW
(*Salix reticulata*)

Description. Mat-forming alpine willow no more than 4 inches tall. Leaves roundish, dark green above and whitish below, with a strong, netlike vein network.
Distribution. Alpine areas.
Remarks. There are several small alpine willow species with "trunks" no more than an inch in diameter.

WILD ROSE
(*Rosa woodsii*)

Description. Five-petaled, pink, fragrant flowers. Fruit looks like a small apple and called a rose hip; occurs in autumn. Prickles of different sizes. Pinnately compound leaves.
Distribution. Aspen groves and riparian areas.
Remarks. There are two species of roses in the park, *Rosa woodsii* and *Rosa acicularis*, or prickly rose. Prickly rose has prickles nearly the same size over entire stem.

Wild rose.

SNOWBERRY
(Symphoricarpos oreophilus)

Description. Low, much-branched shrub with grayish, round leaves. Small, white, tubular flowers. Fruit a white berry.
Distribution. Open slopes of montane zone.
Remarks. Often reproduces by vegetative root runners.

RIVER BIRCH
(Betula occidentalis)

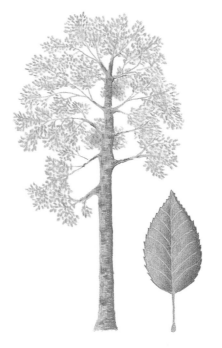

Description. Graceful, multistemmed shrub or small tree to 25 feet. Smooth, reddish brown bark with horizontal lenticels. Leaves ovate and serrate (toothed), yellow in autumn.
Distribution. Along rivers in montane zone.
Remarks. Often called water birch.

DWARF or BOG BIRCH
(Betula glandulosa)

Description. Shrublike, seldom more than 6 feet tall, though usually smaller. Much branched. Small, roundish leaves with toothed margins turn orange-red in autumn.
Distribution. In wet meadows, subalpine to alpine areas.
Remarks. This birch is one of the major species found on the tundra in Alaska.

MOUNTAIN ALDER
(Alnus tenuifolia)

Description. Shrublike tree with spreading, multibranched trunk. Bark gray. Leaves have large veins and are double toothed. Female catkins are conelike and persist through winter.
Distribution. Common along streams.
Remarks. Lacks bright autumn colors; leaves turn brown in autumn and drop.

MYRTLE BLUEBERRY
(Vaccinium myrtillus)

Description. Small shrub, less than a foot high. Alternate branching. Ovate leaves. Brown stems. Blue-black berries.
Distribution. Understory of subalpine forests, particularly under spruce.
Remarks. Fruit is edible and sweet.

RED HUCKLEBERRY
(*Vaccinium scoparium*)

Description. Low, lacy shrub, usually less than a foot high. Green, angled branching. Tiny, green leaves. Fruit small, red berry.
Distribution. Understory of subalpine forest, particularly lodgepole and spruce forest.
Remarks. Sometimes called grouse whortleberry.

FRINGED SAGEBRUSH
(*Artemisia frigida*)

Description. Very small sagebrush with silvery fringed leaves. Slender racemes of yellowish flowers that hang downward from stem.
Distribution. Abundant among rocks all the way to alpine.
Remarks. Fringed sagebrush is found north to Alaska. Another species, mountain big sagebrush (*Artemisia tridentata*), is found in a few places east of the Divide around Deer Mountain, Horseshoe Park, and Glacier Basin. Also found near Grand Lake.

Ferns

BRITTLE FERN
(*Cystopteris fragilis*)

Description. Small fern. Tapering fronds, twice pinnate. Stipes very brittle and will break off easily.
Distribution. Most widely distributed fern in Rocky Mountain National Park. Found in moist crevices and cliffs at all altitudes, even the summit of Specimen Mountain.
Remarks. Appears early in spring and withers as soil dries out.

Bracken fern and aspen in the Glacier Gorge. In autumn, bracken fern turns yellowish red in color.

BRACKEN FERN
(Pteridium aquilinum)

Description. Coarse, stout fern 1 to 4 feet high, with large, triangular fronds.
Distribution. Open areas in montane zone; often invades after a fire. Abundant on the aptly named Fern Lake Trail.
Remarks. After frost in autumn, turns a rusty red color, making it conspicuous among other vegetation.

Grasses

BLUE GRAMA GRASS
(Bouteloua gracilis)

Description. Bunchgrass typically a foot high, with spikelets all on one side of the rachis (stem), making it look like a flag flying in the breeze. Blue-green leaves (blades).

Distribution. Common in meadows up to 8,500 feet.

Remarks. A warm-season grass, doesn't start to green up until June.

NEEDLE and THREAD GRASS
(Stipa comata)

Description. Stem about 2 feet high. Spikelet has a pointed, needlelike seed with a long, threadlike awn.

Distribution. Meadow areas in the montane zone.

Remarks. The long, threadlike awn is attached to the seed and twists in response to moisture, helping to drive the seed into the ground.

MOUNTAIN MUHLY
(Muhlenbergia montana)

Description. Bunchgrass, densely tufted, mostly culms (stems) up to 1 to 2 feet tall. Short-branched panicle 2 to 6 inches long. Threadlike awn.
Distribution. Dry, open parks in ponderosa pine montane zone.
Remarks. In many areas outside of Rocky Mountain National Park, this species has been replaced by blue grama as a consequence of livestock overgrazing.

TUFTED HAIRGRASS
(Deschampsia cespitosa)

Description. Medium to tall bunchgrass. Culms (stems) in dense tufts 2 to 4 feet tall. Leaves are pointed and stiff. Purplish flower cluster has feathery appearance.
Distribution. Moist meadows.
Remarks. Tends to be found in areas with deep snow.

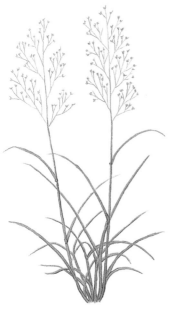

Flowers

WESTERN SHOOTING STAR
(*Dodecatheon pulchellum*)

Description. Cluster of rocket-shaped, pinkish flowers with blackish anthers hanging downward on a leafless stalk. Leaves in a basal rosette.
Distribution. Early-season bloomer that follows snowmelt upward. Wet meadows in the montane and subalpine zone. Abundant along the Dream Lake Trail.
Remarks. Sometimes this flower is so thick, it colors meadows pink.

JACOB'S LADDER
(*Polemonium pulcherrimum* var. *delicatum*)

Description. Light blue flowers. Fernlike leaves consist of ovate leaflets on two-ranked stem suggesting a ladder, hence its name.
Distribution. One of the most common plants of dry, open areas in the understory of spruce forest.
Remarks. Very common near timberline where the spruce forest is broken into islands of stunted timber.

PIPSISSEWA
(*Chimaphila umbellata*)

Description. Dark green, stiff, glossy, roundish leaves in basal whorl. Flowers on a slender stem with nodding round, pink flowers.
Distribution. In deep shade in the montane and subalpine forests up to 11,000 feet.
Remarks. Very fragrant flowers.

RED COLUMBINE
(Aquilegia elegantula)

Description. Plant up to 2 feet tall. Red sepals and yellow-petaled, drooping flowers. Leaves mainly basal, divided in two to three lobes.
Distribution. Moist places in forests on the western slope.
Remarks. Hummingbirds are attracted to the red, nectar-rich flowers.

BLUE COLUMBINE
(Aquilegia caerulea)

Description. Showy, blue and white flowers, 2 to 3 inches across, with long, slender spurs. Plant up to 2 feet tall. Leaves compound and deeply cleft, mostly basal.
Distribution. Rockpiles and in forests, including aspen groves from montane through subalpine up to about 11,500 feet.
Remarks. State flower of Colorado.

Blue columbine.

WESTERN BISTORT
(Polygonum bistortoides)

Description. Plant 8 to 16 inches tall. Dense spike of tiny, white flowers, sometimes tinged pinkish. Narrow, mostly basal leaves.
Distribution. One of the most common flowers in meadows from montane up through subalpine areas.
Remarks. Alpine bistort *(Polygonum viviparum)* is a smaller version of this plant that is common in the alpine areas of Rocky Mountain National Park.

FAIRY PRIMROSE
(Primula angustifolia)

Description. Alpine plant only 2 to 4 inches high. Rose-purple flowers with yellow centers.
Distribution. Grows among the sheltered rocks of boulder fields in alpine areas.
Remarks. One of the first alpine plants to flower.

ALPINE PHLOX
(Phlox pulvinata)

Description. Cushionlike plant with opposite linear leaves on short stem. Flowers have five very pale blue or white petals on leafless stem.
Distribution. Rocky alpine areas.
Remarks. This plant forms matlike islands of color on rocky, well-drained soils.

RYDBERGIA
or ALPINE SUNFLOWER
(*Hymenoxys grandiflora*)

Description. Bright yellow, composite flower 2 to 4 inches across on hairy, 6-inch-long stems. Leaves and stems covered with soft, white hairs. The yellow ray flowers, which resemble petals, have three notches on the tips.
Distribution. Rocky alpine areas.
Remarks. This plant dies after blooming only once. These flowers track the sun, and it's not unusual to see thousands of this species on a ridge, all facing the same direction toward the sun, as if worshipping its warmth.

Alpine sunflower.

SNOWBANK BUTTERCUP
(Ranunculus adoneus)

Description. Bright yellow flowers 1 to 1½ inches across. Leaves dissected in narrow leaflets.
Distribution. In subalpine and alpine meadows.
Remarks. This early-blooming flower often pokes up through snowbanks or grows along the edge of a melting snowbank, hence its common name. There are more than a half dozen other buttercups in Rocky Mountain National Park.

MARSH MARIGOLD
(Caltha leptosepala)

Description. Leaves, all basal, are 1 to 4 inches long, with a heart-shaped base. Flowers are white, sometimes with bluish cast. Yellow anthers create a yellow center.
Distribution. Wet, marshy areas in subalpine and alpine zones. Often blooms near the snowmelt from snowfields.
Remarks. Elk love this plant and consume large quantities.

ROCK JASMINE
(Androsace chamaejasme)

Description. Cushionlike plant. Rosette of small, hairy leaves, umbel of white flowers borne on slender, 1- to 2-inch-tall leafless stalk.
Distribution. Rocky alpine areas.
Remarks. Flowers look something like white forget-me-nots.

MOUNTAIN LUPINE
(Lupinus argenteus)

Description. Palmate, compound leaves with five to nine leaflets. Flowers a blue raceme, sometimes slightly bicolored blue and white. In the pea family and produces a seedpod that looks like a peapod.
Distribution. Upper montane and subalpine zones.
Remarks. There are several different lupine species in Rocky Mountain National Park. Elk consume the flowers and seedpods.

YARROW
(Achillea lanulosa)

Description. Flat-topped cluster of small, white flowers. Height 1 to 3 feet. Numerous leaves pinnately dissected and have a fernlike appearance.
Distribution. Along roadsides and in meadows.
Remarks. Has a strong odor, and when consumed by dairy cattle, gives milk a disagreeable taste.

HEARTLEAF ARNICA
(Arnica cordifolia)

Description. Large, usually solitary, 3-inch, yellow blossom. Basal leaves are heart-shaped, 2 to 3 inches wide. Leaves and stem slightly hairy.
Distribution. Moist montane and subalpine forests.
Remarks. Flower used as a drug and can be used to treat wounds.

WYOMING PAINTBRUSH
(Castilleja linariaefolia)

Description. Brushlike flowers with red calyx and bracts and green corolla. Narrow, grasslike leaves.
Distribution. Dry slopes of the montane.
Remarks. There are three red paintbrushes in Rocky Mountain National Park. The other two, rosy paintbrush and scarlet paintbrush, are found in moist areas in the subalpine and alpine areas. Paintbrushes are semiparasitic, with roots penetrating the roots of other plants, which then supply some of the paintbrush's food needs.

CHIMING BELLS
or TALL BLUEBELLS
(Mertensia ciliata)

Description. Stems over 1 foot tall. Veiny leaves and pendant, bell-shaped, blue blossoms. Buds sometimes pinkish.
Distribution. Abundant along subalpine meadows and streamsides.
Remarks. There are four similar-looking species of bluebells, including chiming bells, in Rocky Mountain National Park; two species are found in the alpine, and the remaining one is a plant of the lower montane.

COW PARSNIP
(Heracleum lanatum)

Description. Large, stout plant up to 6 feet tall. Large, compound, broad leaves in three-lobed leaflets. Numerous small, white-pinkish flowers in a broad, foot-wide umbel blossom.
Distribution. Moist woods and stream-banks of the montane and subalpine zones.
Remarks. Elk and black bears consume this plant with relish.

MOUNTAIN AVENS
(Dryas octopetala)

Description. Dwarf, mat-forming plant of alpine areas. Large, dark, glossy, leathery leaves with cream-colored 1-inch blossoms with eight petals. Hairy achenes (seeds) that look like a mop of gray whiskers in August.
Distribution. Dry alpine areas.
Remarks. An arctic-alpine plant that is very common in the tundra of Alaska. Its rolled leaf margins and leathery, thick leaves reduce moisture loss in the drying winds of the alpine zone.

Alpine avens.

ALPINE AVENS
(Geum rossii)

Description. Dwarf, mat-forming plant. Bright yellow, five-petaled flowers. Pinnately divided, fernlike, dark green, mostly basal leaves.
Distribution. The most common alpine plant in Rocky Mountain National Park, blooming from late June onward.
Remarks. Leaves turn reddish bronze in autumn.

FISH

Straddling the Continental Divide, Rocky Mountain National Park lies at the headwaters of a number of rivers, including the mighty Colorado and the Platte. There are an estimated 147 lakes and 421 miles of streams in the park. Nevertheless, as a headwaters region, most park streams are small and are full of cascades, waterfalls, and rapids that act as barriers for fish movement. Originally, many of the upper parts of the park's streams were barren of fish. Fish were also originally absent from all or most of the small high-elevation lakes (historic records are unclear about the exact status of every lake).

Due to the cold water and the small size of streams and lakes, the most abundant fish species are members of the trout and sucker family that thrive under such conditions. Growth is slow, and a sixteen-inch fish is considered large, with the largest fish ever taken a cutthroat trout caught in Lake Nakoni that was twenty-five inches in length.

Fish stocking, which began even before Rocky Mountain was declared a national park, was done to increase angling opportunities. In 1969, the park implemented a no-stocking policy. At that time, approximately fifty-nine lakes had fish maintained by natural reproduction or stocking. With the termination of stocking, the number of lakes holding reproducing fish populations dropped to forty-seven.

Fish were stocked with no regard to the existing fish populations or the impact on the aquatic ecosystems. For example, though six species of trout are now found in the park, only two, the greenback cutthroat and Colorado River cutthroat, are native. Some fish that were introduced, such as the Atlantic salmon, did not survive. Others persisted, including the brook, brown, rainbow, and Yellowstone cutthroat trout, none of which are native to Colorado or, in the case of brook trout and brown trout, even to the West. Both lake trout and kokanee salmon, a landlocked sockeye salmon, have been stocked in Grand Lake just outside Rocky Mountain National Park.

Ironically, one reason native fish are in trouble is as a consequence of fish stocking. Competition and hybridization with non-native trout has pushed the greenback cutthroat and Colorado River cutthroat trout both closer to the edge of extinction. Only now are we beginning to appreciate that fish stocking has many negative effects upon native fish and invertebrates.

In 1973, when the greenback cutthroat trout was listed under the Endangered Species Act, there were only two known populations of the fish thought to exist in the world. One was in the upper headwaters of the South Fork of the Poudre River, just north of Rocky Mountain National Park, and the other was in Como Creek near Nederlands. The total estimated world population of the fish at this time was thought to number no more than 2,000. Since 1973, a major restoration program has established greenback cutthroat trout in twenty-four sites within Rocky Mountain National Park and fifty-two sites in Colorado. Thus the greenback is back from the brink of extinction.

The evolution of cutthroat trout is a fascinating story. The present distribution of the cutthroat trout in all its varieties is largely a consequence of Pleistocene glaciation, which rearranged the hydrology of the West and permitted the colonization of many water bodies by the species. There are now fourteen to fifteen recognized subspecies of cutthroat trout distributed around the West (the exact number is disputed among scientists). The cutthroat genetic line first split from a common ancestor of the rainbow trout, then split again into three branches: the Yellowstone, the westslope, and the coastal cutthroat trout. The Yellowstone cutthroat variety gave rise to all the subspecies now found in Colorado, including the Colorado River cutthroat and the greenback cutthroat.

The early form of Yellowstone cutthroat trout originally reached the interior West by swimming up the Snake River. It eventually reached the headwaters in Idaho and Wyoming. During the last ice age, barrier falls developed on the Snake River that isolated the Yellowstone form of cutthroat in the upper river, separating it from other cutthroat trout and from rainbow trout that colonized the Columbia River drainage following the last ice age.

Yellowstone cutthroat trout.

These early precursors of today's Yellowstone cutthroat trout were then able to swim up the Snake River and cross the Continental Divide into both the Yellowstone and Green River drainages. The headwaters of both of these rivers lie close together just south of Yellowstone Park. The Green is a tributary of the Colorado River. From the headwaters of the Green, the future Colorado River cutthroat trout migrated downstream, following the Green into the Colorado River. Once in the Colorado, it swam back upstream toward the headwater region, including the Upper Colorado River in what is now Rocky Mountain National Park. Over time, this fish became what we know as the Colorado River cutthroat trout.

Once in the headwaters of the Colorado River, some of these cutthroat trout crossed the Continental Divide into the South Platte and Arkansas River drainages. Isolated in these rivers, these fish evolved into the greenback cutthroat trout.

It is sometimes possible to know when you have crossed from the Yellowstone and Snake River drainages into the Green merely by examining the fish. Yellowstone cutthroat are rather dull in coloration, whereas the Colorado River basin fish sport brilliant colors. Spawning Colorado cutthroat trout have bright crimson bellies and brassy yellow sides. The greenback cutthroat trout is also very brightly colored.

The major difference between these two cutthroat trout native to Rocky Mountain National Park is the size and distribution of spots. The greenback has very large black spots on its tail and sides; the spots of the Colorado cutthroat are smaller and less abundant on the forward portion of the fish.

Some readers may be wondering how fish can get across the Continental Divide. It's actually not that unusual for tributaries of two great river systems to have common sources in a low-gradient pass. For example, Summit Lake on Marias Pass, just south of Glacier National Park in Montana, has two outlets. One flows to the Flathead River and ultimately the Pacific Ocean, while the other outlet flows via the Two Medicine River to the Missouri River and eventually the Mississippi. Even today, a fish from west of the Continental Divide can swim over the Divide and enter the Missouri drainage or vice versa. Similar situations have existed in the past in other river drainages as well.

Rocky Mountain National Park is home to two of the four cutthroat trout originally native to Colorado: the greenback and the Colorado River cutthroats. (The other two native species are the Rio Grande cutthroat and the extinct yellowfin cutthroat.) The three cutthroat subspecies remaining in the state have suffered substantial reductions in their original distribution and numbers, both in the park and in the rest of their geographical range. Greenback cutthroats were once reduced to just five small populations isolated in the headwaters of a few tiny creeks. The Colorado River cutthroat has fared slightly better, only because its original range was so much broader, encompassing the entire Green and Upper Colorado drainages, including major parts of Utah, Wyoming, and Colorado.

There are a number of reasons for the decline of the cutthroat trout. They were partially victims of overfishing. Throughout their range, and particularly in tourist destinations like Rocky Mountain National Park, there were essentially no restrictions on fishing. It was common for people to catch twenty-five to fifty fish a day and keep them all. In small streams like those in the park, it's relatively easy to take most of the adult fish from the stream.

A more lasting impact has come from habitat loss. Aridity is common in much of the West, and many rivers and streams are exploited to provide irrigation water for agriculture and domestic uses. Despite all the golf courses and lawns of Kentucky bluegrass along the Front Range cities, agriculture is still largely responsible for most water habitat loss. In Colorado, urban use consumes 5 percent of the state's water, agriculture uses 85 percent, and the rest is divided between rural water supply and industry. In Colorado, as in most of the West, irrigation is mainly used to grow hay and other crops to feed cattle, not humans.

Dewatering of streams occurs even in Rocky Mountain National Park. The "big ditch" dug along the face of the Never Summer Range captures water that would otherwise flow into the Colorado River and sends this water to the Cache la Poudre drainage and ultimately to agricultural irrigation on the plains. In addition, a number of lakes in the park are dammed and form storage reservoirs for irrigation outside the park.

Livestock grazing has also directly affected fish habitat. Cattle breeds on western ranches were originally from moist Eurasia woodlands. They seek out moist areas with lush vegetation, which in the West are primarily found along the shores of streams and lakes. Trampling and heavy grazing by cattle have destroyed the stream channels and streamside vegetation of the majority of rivers and streams in the West, leading to increased sedimentation, channel widening, and loss of protective cover and shade—all of which negatively effect trout and other fish.

Fortunately, livestock is no longer grazed in the park, but the animals continue to degrade fish habitat in most of the West, including areas within the natural ranges of both the Colorado River and greenback cutthroat trout.

Another major factor that negatively affects native fish is hybridization. Cutthroat trout easily hybridize with each other, as well as with the closely related rainbow trout. Cut-bow crosses are common in Rocky Mountain National Park. Hybridization with other cutthroats, such as the Yellowstone cutthroat, has also genetically polluted the park's native trout.

All these factors have practically eliminated cutthroat trout from much of the West where they were originally found. Indeed, of the fourteen to fifteen recognized subspecies of cutthroat trout found in the West, only one, the coastal cutthroat, is not in any jeopardy over most of its range. Of the others, most are either listed or candidates for listing under the Endangered Species Act. The greenback cutthroat trout, originally found throughout the upper reaches of the South Platte and Arkansas Rivers, was at one time thought to be down to a single small population. To prevent extinction, the fish was listed in 1973 as endangered under the federal Endangered Species Act. A recovery effort was begun, which, among other things, turned up several more small isolated populations of the fish. As a consequence, in 1978 the greenback was downlisted to the less serious category of threatened.

Much of the recovery effort has focused on Rocky Mountain National Park because it was once the stronghold of the greenback cutthroat trout and because conflicts with cattle grazing and dewatering for irrigation have been less of an issue here. Today greenback trout are found in more than two dozen park waters and are holding their own.

To restore the park's native cutthroats, the Park Service, along with the U.S. Fish and Wildlife Service and Colorado Fish and Game, have embarked on a greenback trout recovery program. A number of streams and lakes with natural barriers, such as waterfalls, downstream have been poisoned to eliminate non-native trout. Then these waters are stocked with greenback trout. Thus far, this has been successful in pulling the fish back from the brink of extinction, although it is still a long way from recovering most of its native range in the state. Nevertheless, at this point, the fish is abundant enough within the park to support a limited greenback cutthroat trout sport fishery.

The Colorado River cutthroat has fared slightly better than the greenback, largely because its original range was so much broader. Yet its numbers continue to decline, and it too may be added to the list of species protected under the Endangered Species Act.

Classification of Trout

There are a number of native and non-native fish collectively called trout within Rocky Mountain National Park. Very few of them are really "trout," however. Recent genetic DNA work has changed our view of the West's native fish. All trout endemic to the western United States are now considered members of the Pacific salmon family, in the genus *Oncorhynchus*. For example, both rainbow trout and cutthroat trout are now considered Pacific salmon, and their Latin name has been changed from *Salmo* to *Oncorhynchus* to reflect this new status. Thus the rainbow trout is now classified as *Oncorhynchus mykiss*, the Colorado River cutthroat is *Oncorhynchus clarki pleuriticus*, and the greenback cutthroat trout is now *Onchorhynchus clarki stomias*. All three fish are found in Rocky Mountain National Park today. The two cutthroat species are native to the park, and the rainbow trout has been successfully introduced.

Trout from the Atlantic Ocean basin, including the brown trout (*Salmo trutta*) and the Atlantic salmon, are members of the Atlantic salmon genus *Salmo*. Brown trout is a European species that has been widely introduced across North America, including Rocky Mountain National Park.

The differences between Pacific salmon/trout and Atlantic salmon/ trout are relatively minor. Members of the Pacific salmon group have a toothed vomer, a bone that lies in the center roof of the mouth, and those in the Atlantic salmon group have teeth on the anterior end of the vomer. The other major difference is in the spotting. Pacific salmon have black spots on a silver or crimson background; the Atlantic salmon group lacks black spots but may have other colors, including white and red.

To further confuse the matter, brook trout (*Salvelinus fontinalis*) aren't trout, but char, along with lake trout and bull trout. All char are within the genus *Salvelinus*. The brook trout is the only char/trout species successfully introduced into Rocky Mountain National Park.

Species Accounts
Trout

GREENBACK
CUTTHROAT TROUT
(Oncorhynchus clarki stomias)

Description. Red slash on each side of throat. Elongated body with short head. Mouth large. Teeth on jaws, vomer, and tongue. Dark brown dorsally, with bright red, orange, or yellowish sides. Often has pinkish or crimson gill covers. Large, black spots densely distributed on caudal fin and less dense on rest of body. Black spots on body much larger than those of Colorado cutthroat trout; typically the largest spots of any subspecies of cutthroat trout.

Distribution. Found in the following lakes and streams: South Fork of the Poudre River, Hunters Creek, Upper Hutcheson Lake, Mid Hutcheson Lake, North Fork of the Big Thompson, Hidden Valley, Bear Lake, West Creek, Ouzel Lake, Loomis Lake, Fern Lake, Fern Creek, Odessa Lake, Lawn Lake, Big Crystal Lake, Roaring River, Lost Lake, Lower Hutcheson Lake, Sandbeach Reservoir, Pear Reservoir, Cony Creek, Lake Louise, Husted Lake, Spruce Lake, Sandbeach Creek, and Dream Lake.

Remarks. Typically does not spawn until late June or even into July. Eggs tend to hatch more rapidly than those of other trout as an adaptation to its cold, high-elevation habitat. Originally native to the Arkansas and South Platte Rivers and tributaries, including in Rocky Mountain National Park. Nearly extirpated throughout its range and by mid-1970s reduced to five remote locations in the state. It was listed as an endangered species in 1973 and protected under the Endangered Species Act. It is still rare and is now considered threatened, a slightly less protective status.

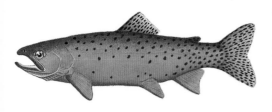

COLORADO RIVER CUTTHROAT TROUT
(Oncorhynchus clarki pleuriticus)

Description. Red slash on either side of throat. Body elongated with short head. Large mouth. Dark brownish back, with crimson red, orange, or yellowish sides. Often has pinkish or crimson gill covers. Black spotting concentrated toward tail but also found over rest of body.

Distribution. Native to the Upper Colorado River drainage in Rocky Mountain National Park. Found in Timber Lake, Paradise Creek, Solitude Lake, Ten Lakes Park, North Inlet, Ypsilon Lake, Willow Creek, Fourth Lake, and Nanita Lake.

Remarks. Once found in most clearwater tributaries of the Green and Colorado River systems above the Grand Canyon in Utah, Wyoming, and Colorado. The Colorado River cutthroat is slightly more abundant than the greenback cutthroat trout; nevertheless, it is in serious decline across its range from habitat loss due to irrigation, livestock grazing, logging, and hybridization with other trout.

YELLOWSTONE CUTTHROAT TROUT
(*Oncorhynchus clarki bouvieri*)

Description. Red slash on either side of throat. Elongated body with short head. Blunt snout and large mouth. Yellowish brown body with brown-tan fins. Often has crimson or pinkish gill covers. Black spots on body, concentrated toward the tail. Spots smaller in size than those of either the Colorado River or greenback cutthroat trout. Up to 24 inches, but most considerably smaller.

Distribution. Originally found in the Upper Snake and Upper Yellowstone River drainages, particularly in Yellowstone National Park, but stocked widely in the western United States. Fish in Rocky Mountain National Park are the result of stocking.

Remarks. Beginning near the turn of the century and continuing through the 1940s, up to 400,000 Yellowstone cutthroat fry were stocked annually in Rocky Mountain National Park. The natural range of the Yellowstone cutthroat has shrunk so dramatically that it may soon be added to the endangered species list. The Yellowstone cutthroat trout is one of the source fish from which Colorado River and greenback cutthroat trout evolved. Like all cutthroat trout, the Yellowstone is a late-spring spawner, making it vulnerable to early-summer irrigation dewatering, which can leave trout eggs high and dry.

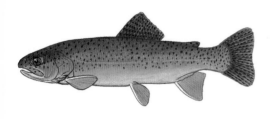

RAINBOW TROUT
(*Oncorhynchus mykiss*)

Description. Body elongated, with short head and large, rounded mouth. Back dark green to blue-green, with silvery sides. A distinct bright red or pink lateral stripe runs from gills to tail. Unlike the cutthroat trout, which tends to have relatively few spots in the forward part of the body and sides, the rainbow has small, black spots profusely distributed over the entire body except the belly, with head, body, fins, and tail all covered with spots.

Distribution. Native to Pacific coastal streams west of the Continental Divide and now widely introduced throughout the world. Three lakes—Jewel, Mills, and Spruce—support rainbow trout. Rainbow trout are also found in the Fall and Big Thompson Rivers.

Remarks. Rainbow trout originally evolved in the Sacramento–San Joaquin River drainage of California and subsequently spread around the Pacific Basin. There are two forms—coastal rainbow and inland, which is known as redband trout. Rainbow trout were recently reclassified as members of the Pacific salmon family.

BROWN TROUT
(Salmo trutta)

Description. Body elongated; relatively large head and mouth compared with those of other trout. Brown to olive green above, with yellow belly. Black dots, particularly on back, and red spots on the sides. Average size is 12 to 18 inches but can reach weights of 40 pounds or more.
Distribution. Originally native to Europe but widely stocked throughout the world, including Rocky Mountain National Park. Seldom found above 9,000 feet. Most abundant in Colorado, Big Thompson, and Fall Rivers.
Remarks. A fall spawner, hence has suffered less from irrigation dewatering in areas where it is severe (significant dewatering doesn't occur in the park) than native fish such as the cutthroat trout, which is a late-spring–early-summer spawner.

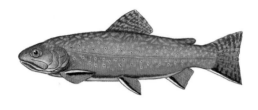

BROOK TROUT
(Salvelinus fontinalis)

Description. Body elongated with a moderately forked tail. Blunt head and large mouth. Body dark green above with white. Belly of spawning males turns bright crimson. White-and-black-edged anal, pelvic, and pectoral fins. Red-pink spots bordered by blue on sides. Back has wormlike markings that become spots on sides. Most brook trout in Rocky Mountain do not exceed a foot in length.

Distribution. Native to eastern North America but stocked widely in the West. Probably the most abundant fish in the park. Does particularly well in lakes and high-elevation streams. About a dozen lakes and some streams contain brook trout, including Mirror, Glass, Poudre, and Verna. Also found in the upper Colorado, Big Thompson, and Fall Rivers.

Remarks. Really a char, not a trout. Other members of the char family include lake trout and bull trout. Despite its name, the brook trout lives in lakes as well. Indeed, it does particularly well in high mountain lakes. A fall spawner, the brook trout can spawn in shallows along the edges of lakes where springs bubble up, so it can thrive even in lakes without access to streams. Very common in beaver ponds. Often outcompetes native fish such as cutthroat trout. Lakes often become overpopulated with small and stunted fish.

Brook trout are not native to Colorado but are widely distributed as a result of stocking programs.

Suckers

Suckers are bottom-dwelling fish related to minnows. Their fleshy lips are oriented downward for bottom feeding. The anal fin is situated far back on the fish.

MOUNTAIN SUCKER
(Catostomus platyrhynchus)

Description. Body slender, with roundish fins. Lateral notch on lips. Grayish above shading to yellow or red below, with blotches over body. Breeding males have bright red lateral stripe. Seldom over 6 inches.
Distribution. Widely distributed in the West, but primarily west of the Continental Divide. In Rocky Mountain National Park, found only in west-slope drainages.
Remarks. Feeds on algae and small aquatic insects.

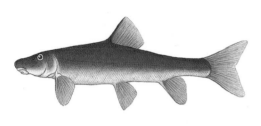

WESTERN LONGNOSE SUCKER
(Catostomus catostomus griseus)

Description. Slender body; flat, long snout. Lips fleshy and lack lateral notch. Grayish above with white to yellow on belly. Breeding males sometimes have red lateral stripe. Length up to 24 inches.
Distribution. Widely distributed in North America and native to South Platte drainage in Rocky Mountain National Park. Prefers cold water and is sometimes found in lakes.
Remarks. Spring (June in Rocky Mountain National Park) spawner, often forming spawning aggregations.

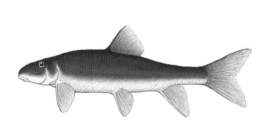

WHITE SUCKER
(Catostomus commersoni suckii)

Description. Body and anal fin elongated. Lips have no lateral notch. Grayish above, fading to white on the belly. Breeding males are bronze colored. Young fish have three distinct dark spots on sides.
Distribution. Found from Rockies to Atlantic Ocean. Native to east-slope waters in Rocky Mountain National Park, but may have been introduced to west slope. Thrives in streams and lakes alike. Prefers clear waters.
Remarks. Aggregates in spawning groups. When spawning, males turn nearly black on back.

Sculpin

Sculpin are small, spiny-rayed fish with flattened heads. They are found under rocks in streams.

MOTTLED SCULPIN
(*Cottus bairdi punctulatus*)

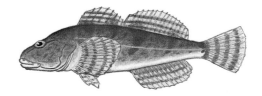

Description. Small fish, typically not more than 4 to 6 inches. Body slender and flattened laterally. Prominent spiny dorsal fin. Dorsal fin tapers toward the tail. Mouth large with broad, flat snout. Body brownish gray, mottled with darker blotches. Belly whitish, often with yellow or blue cast.

Distribution. Widely distributed across North America in clear, cold streams. In Rocky Mountain National Park, restricted to the west slope (Colorado River drainage).

Remarks. Hides under rocks and among gravel by day and mostly forages at night. Feeds mostly on aquatic insects.

AMPHIBIANS
AND REPTILES

It is thought that amphibians preceded reptiles in evolution. Amphibians made the move from water onto land but nevertheless remain tied to water in some ways. Reptiles took this a step further and severed the connection to water altogether, evolving to live entirely on dry land; however, not all reptiles live out of water.

Amphibian is derived from *amphi*, a Greek word that means "double," and *bios*, meaning "life." It refers to the aquatic and terrestrial states of the amphibian. Amphibian eggs lack a shell to protect them from dehydration, thus amphibians must lay their eggs in moist locations or water. The larvae develop in water, then are able to live at least part of the time out of water. Reptiles, on the other hand, lay shelled eggs much like those of chickens and other birds. This allows them to live far from water and is one reason reptiles are abundant in desert regions.

Like their eggs, amphibians have thin skin that must remain moist. Reptiles, on the other hand, have dry, scaly skin.

Amphibians and reptiles are cold-blooded creatures. As a consequence, they are greatly affected by the surrounding air temperatures. The high elevation, often arid conditions, and generally cold temperatures that dominate Rocky Mountain National Park for much of the year make the park a less-than-ideal environment for these animals. Not surprisingly, only six species are reported for the park. All are generalists adapted to harsh environments, with large ranges over the region.

Species Accounts

Exercise caution when interpreting species descriptions. All colors, sizes, and other information are approximate to give a general idea of the size of the species or its color patterns. The age, size, even the light the animal is being viewed in can affect things, such as apparent coloration. Use all descriptions as a general guide, but recognize that great variability exists in nature.

TIGER SALAMANDER
(Ambystoma tigrinum)

Description. Length including tail 9 inches. Flattened head with two small, protruding eyes. Color varies from olive to nearly black. Yellow blotches or stripes on side give rise to its common name, tiger.

Distribution. One of the most widely distributed salamanders in the West. In Rocky Mountain National Park, usually found in or near fishless ponds, streams, and wetlands.

Remarks. Many species prey on tiger salamanders, including coyotes, trout, great blue herons, river otters, and bobcats. These salamanders sometimes make overland migrations during spring mating season.

WESTERN TOAD
(Bufo boreas)

Description. Length 2 to 5 inches. Warty skin. Olive-brown with white stripe down the center of back. Belly lighter and mottled. Pupils of eyes horizontal. Travel by short hops or walking rather than long jumps like frogs.

Distribution. From 7,000 to 11,000 feet, but usually above 9,000 feet near warm, shallow water bodies with adjacent meadows.

Remarks. Bumps on back are poison glands, which excrete a toxin that discourages some predators. These toads hibernate in burrows. Breed in shallow lakes, beaver ponds, wetlands, and seeps.

WESTERN CHORUS FROG
(Pseudacris triseriata)

Description. Small. Length 1½ inches. Slender body; almost no webbing on hind feet. Color can be light tan or greenish. Three dark stripes on back, which may be interrupted or incomplete on some individuals. Lateral stripe on either side passes through eye, giving a masked appearance.
Distribution. Wet meadows or grass along streams. Breeds in shallow lakes or even wet, grassy meadows.
Remarks. Loud breeding call in spring gives rise to its common name, chorus frog. Most calling occurs at night.

NORTHERN LEOPARD FROG
(Rana pipiens)

Description. Length 4 inches. Smooth skin. Generally green, though sometimes brown, upperparts with white belly. Large, black spots with light borders around each spot, giving rise to its common name, leopard frog.
Distribution. Prefers grass-sedge shores of lakes and ponds.
Remarks. One of the most widespread amphibians in the United States, but declining over much of its range in the West. In Colorado, appears to have been extirpated from 85 percent of its former range. In Rocky Mountain National Park, has seriously declined as well, despite the existence of good wetland habitat.

WOOD FROG
(Rana sylvatica)

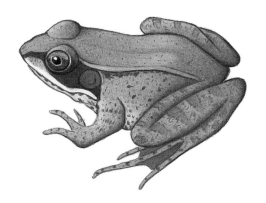

Description. Length 3 inches. Flattened body with pointed snout but broad head. Upperparts usually tan but can also be dark brown, while belly is typically white or mottled. Prominent dark mask covers each eye and extends along side of head to just behind eardrum. Toes are only slightly webbed.

Distribution. Ranges far from water, but likes damp woodlands. Although a strong swimmer, it spends little time near water except during breeding season.

Remarks. Adapted to cold environments—its range extends into Alaska north of the Arctic Circle. More terrestrial than other frogs. Capable of jumping long distances.

WESTERN TERRESTRIAL GARTER SNAKE
(Thamnophis elegans)

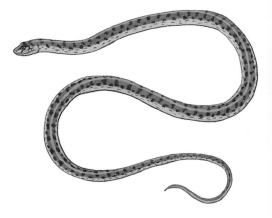

Description. Length to 30 inches. Varies in color, with green, brown, or gray base color. Three yellow stripes run down length of the body—one down the back and two on either side. Rows of dark spots occur between stripes on back or sides.

Distribution. Usually found near water, generally below 10,000 feet.

Remarks. Although they have excellent eyesight, these snakes locate most prey through smell and taste. One experiment found that the garter snake could capture prey and relocate its burrow even with its eyes taped closed.

Birds

Birds are warm-blooded, which allows for activity in all kinds of weather. Maintaining body temperature, especially for smaller species, requires a lightweight, but efficient insulation, provided by feathers. Feathers are remarkably warm, as anyone who has worn a down coat can testify. It is warm-bloodedness that permits birds to live in a high, cold environment like that found in Rocky Mountain National Park. Not surprisingly, Rocky Mountain National Park has far more birds and mammals—both endothermic animal groups—than the cold-blooded reptiles and amphibians.

To sustain flight, birds must be lightweight. Most birds have light, hollow bones, with internal "struts" something like the framework of a house. The skeleton of a pigeon, for example, accounts for 4.4 percent of its total body weight, whereas the skeleton of a comparable-size mammal such as a white rat weighs close to 5.5 percent of its body weight. And the skeleton of the frigate bird, a seabird with a 7-foot wingspread that often glides for miles across the open ocean, weighs less than its feathers. Rather than teeth and strong jaw muscles, birds have lightweight bills. Because of their high energy requirements, as well as the need to remain lightweight, birds tend to eat high-energy, compact foods such as seeds, insects, and fruits rather than the bulkier and heavier grass or leaves.

Birds are the only class of vertebrates with no members that bear live young. Instead, they lay eggs, and most of the development of the babies occurs outside the female's body. Carrying around developing young inside the mother's body would severely impede flight.

Birds have huge flight muscles. In strong flying birds like the pigeon, these breast muscles may account for two-fifths of the total body weight. To sustain the oxygen supply of these huge muscles, birds have larger hearts and a higher heart rate than other comparable-size animals.

Birding at Rocky Mountain National Park

The bulk of Rocky Mountain National Park contains three habitat zones—montane forest, subalpine forest, and tundra. Birds, being highly mobile, are seen in many different habitats, but they are often associated with specific habitat types. Although the tundra zone may have the most distinctive birds found in the region, such as the white-tailed ptarmigan, the majority of bird species found in the park live or forage in the montane forest zone between 8,000 and 9,500 feet, which is dominated by ponderosa pine, Douglas fir, lodgepole pine, and aspen. The best birding areas are found in the montane zone: the Moraine Park, Upper Beaver Meadows, and Horseshoe Park areas. The subalpine zone lies in the heavy snow belt between 9,500 and 11,000 feet and is dominated by forests of Engelmann spruce and subalpine fir, with an occasional grove of limber pine on rocky substrates. Interspersed among these forests are lush subalpine meadows. The treeless alpine zone occurs above 11,000 feet.

Montane Zone

Species likely to be seen in the ponderosa pine forest include the chipping sparrow, dark-eyed junco, mountain bluebird, mountain chickadee, northern flicker, Steller's jay, western tanager, white-breasted nuthatch, and yellow-rumped warbler. In the Douglas fir forests, in addition to the previous species, you are also likely to encounter the ruby-crowned kinglet, brown creeper, hermit thrush, and pine siskin. Aspen groves are exceptional places for birding, and species one may spy there include the tree swallow, warbling vireo, violet-green swallow, red-naped woodpecker, mountain bluebird, hairy woodpecker, and downy woodpecker.

Some of the best birding areas in this zone are the forest and riparian areas at Beaver Meadows. Here you might see violet-green and tree swallows, the mountain chickadee, ruby-crowned kinglet, mountain bluebird, dusky flycatcher, Hammond's flycatcher, Steller's jay, and Wilson's warbler.

In the ponderosa pine and aspen forest along the road through Moraine Park toward the Fern Lake trailhead, you might encounter the pygmy nuthatch, mountain chickadee, red crossbill, red-naped and Williamson's sapsuckers, western tanager, pine siskin, chipping sparrow, western wood-pewee, and broad-tailed and rufous hummingbird.

If you wander down to the riparian area along Big Thompson River, which flows through Moraine Park, you may well be treated to glimpses of

Glacier Creek by Alberta Falls. This creek lies in the subalpine zone and offers excellent birding for blue grouse, mountain chickadees, ruby-crowned kinglets, and yellow-rumped warblers, among other species.

the belted kingfisher, dipper, song sparrow, hermit thrush, and Mac-Gillivray and yellow warblers.

Subalpine Zone

Due to its generally cold temperatures and heavy snow cover, fewer birds reside in the subalpine zone. Species you are likely to see include the blue grouse, hermit thrush, mountain chickadee, pine grosbeak, ruby-crowned kinglet, Townsend's solitaire, yellow-rumped warbler, golden-crowned kinglet, olive-sided flycatcher, and dark-eyed junco.

One of the easiest places to access the subalpine forest is one of the many trails that radiate from the Glacier Basin trailhead. Hiking any of these trails, you might see the blue grouse, gray jay, and Clark's nutcracker.

The Trail Ridge Road also climbs up through the subalpine into the alpine zone, offering good birding along the way. Expect to see the Steller's jay and Clark's nutcracker in the forested areas.

Alpine Zone

Few birds live readily in the harsh climatic conditions of the alpine zone. There are, however, a few birds that are specifically adapted to life in the alpine region. These include five species strongly associated with this zone, including the white-tailed ptarmigan, white-crowned sparrow, American pipit, horned lark, and brown-capped rosy finch. You may, however, spy other species, such as the golden eagle and prairie falcon, gliding on the winds.

The easiest access to the alpine zone is from the Trail Ridge Road. If you climb the road from the east, stop when you reach the Forest Canyon overlook, and take some time to do a short hike, looking for white-tailed ptarmigan. Other tundra-nesting birds include the brown-capped rosy finch, American pipit, and horned lark; a good place to see these birds is along the Tundra World Nature Trail. White-crowned sparrows are often seen in the willows growing in pockets along the Trail Ridge Road as well.

When you cross Trail Ridge, you enter the North Fork of the Colorado River Valley. Birding opportunities here are similar to those in the forested valleys on the eastern side of the park; however, when you reach the three big lakes—Grand, Shadow Mountain, and Granby—you may see a few new species, including the osprey, western grebe, pied-billed grebe, and perhaps an occasional bald eagle.

Species Accounts

Some 280 species have been reported for Rocky Mountain National Park and surrounding areas. The species described below breed in the park, are year-round residents, or are relatively common migrants. A complete listing of species recorded in or near the park appears at the end of this book.

Abundance is based upon the bird's relative numbers in suitable habitat. Some species, such as the golden eagle, are fairly common in Rocky Mountain National Park, but golden eagles are not abundant anyplace. Birds' mobility due to flight makes it more difficult to predict where and when one might sight any particular bird species. Distribution as given below is based upon habitat preferences.

Exercise caution when interpreting species descriptions. All colors, sizes, and other information are only approximate to give a general idea of the size of the bird or its color patterns. The colors of birds sometimes change with the season; for instance, breeding birds often have more intense coloration. Most descriptions reflect summer coloration, since that is the time when most people visit Rocky Mountain National Park. The age, size, even the light the bird is being viewed in can affect things like apparent coloration. Use all descriptions as a general guide, but recognize that great variability exists in nature.

Waterfowl

This large group includes ducks, grebes, geese, swans, and loons, all webbed-footed aquatic birds. Thirty-four species of waterfowl are known to occur in or near the park, but only eight are common enough to merit discussion. Most waterfowl are associated with lakes; in particular, large reservoirs such as Shadow Mountain Lake, Lake Granby, and Grand Lake, on the border of the park in the Arapaho National Recreation Area, are excellent sites to observe these birds.

WESTERN GREBE
(Aechmophorus occidentalis)

Description. Length 28 inches. Adults grayish above, white below. Long, thin, white neck. Top half of head, including area surrounding the red eye, is black. Pointed, yellow bill. Lobed toes.
Distribution. Fairly common migrant and summer resident. Lakes and reservoirs. Seen in Shadow Mountain Lake, Grand Lake, and Lake Granby.
Remarks. Strong swimmers, seldom seen on land. Pairs perform a ritualistic breeding dance, running together side by side as they splash across the surface.

GREEN-WINGED TEAL
(Anas crecca)

Description. Length 14 inches. Male has gray sides with white stripe below the shoulder, light brown breast, chestnut brown head with green ear patch behind eye. Green patch on wing. Female mottled brown.
Distribution. Fairly common migrant and summer resident. Marshes, ponds, and reservoirs.
Remarks. A fast-flying, agile duck. Common on the plains, but occasionally found into the mountains. Among the earliest-returning spring waterfowl migrants.

BLUE-WINGED TEAL
(Anas discors)

Description. Length 16 inches. Male brown above, with grayish head and neck. White crescent in front of eye. Wing speculum green with blue patch. Female brownish overall.
Distribution. Fairly common migrant and summer resident. Slow streams, beaver ponds, and marshes.
Remarks. One of the latest duck migrants to arrive in the area. Fast-flying.

MALLARD
(Anas platyrhynchos)

Description. Length 23 inches. Male has metallic green head. Yellow bill. Body gray with brown breast. Blue wing patch edged in white. Female mottled brown with blue wing patch edged in white.
Distribution. Very common summer resident and migrant. Slow streams, beaver ponds, and marshes.
Remarks. Mallards feed "bottoms up," tipping over to feed on insects and aquatic plants in shallow water.

RING-NECKED DUCK
(Aythya collaris)

Description. Length 17 inches. Male has black head, breast, and back. Sides gray. White at base of bill and white stripe on lower part of bill. Female grayish brown.
Distribution. Fairly common migrant and summer resident. Found on larger lakes and reservoirs.
Remarks. Deep-water ducks. Common on big reservoirs. Closely resembles lesser scaup.

LESSER SCAUP
(Aythya affinis)

Description. Length 16 inches. Male has purple-black head and black breast, but grayish white back. Sides pale gray. Blue bill. Female is brown overall, but with white patch at base of the bill.
Distribution. Fairly common migrant and winter resident. Found on ponds, reservoirs, and marshes.
Remarks. Sometimes known as blue bill.

COMMON GOLDENEYE
(Bucephala clangula)

Description. Length 18 inches. Yellow eyes. Male has glossy green head with white patch below eye, white breast, and white wing patches visible in flight during breeding season. Female has grayish body, white neck ring, and reddish brown head with black bill tipped in yellow; the similar mature female Barrow's goldeneye has all-yellow bill.
Distribution. Fairly common resident on open water in winter.
Remarks. Cavity nester, found on ponds and lakes near trees during breeding season. Known as "whistler" because rapid wingbeat creates a high-pitched, whirling noise in flight.

COMMON MERGANSER
(Mergus merganser)

Description. Length 25 inches. Male has metallic green head with narrow, red bill. White breast, neck, sides, and belly. White wing bars visible in flight. Female has grayish body, white breast and chin, and crested chestnut head with narrow, red bill.

Distribution. Fairly common in winter, during migrations, and in summer. Found on lakes and larger rivers.

Remarks. Fish eater. Swims well underwater. Nests in cavities. Splashes across surface of water when attempting to become airborne.

Hawks, Eagles, and Falcons

These birds of prey have sharp talons and hooked bills for tearing meat. In most species, males tend to be smaller than females. There are sixteen species recorded for the park, but only eight are discussed below.

NORTHERN GOSHAWK
(Accipiter gentilis)

Description. Length 26 inches. Grayish blue back and head, with red eye. Underparts gray-white barred with gray. Fluffy, white feathers beneath tail. Immature is brownish.

Distribution. Uncommon year-round resident. Prefers dense conifer forests, particularly spruce-fir, lodgepole pine, and ponderosa pine, but occasionally found in aspen groves.

Remarks. Eats mammals and grouse. Strongly territorial around nest and will attack intruders.

COOPER'S HAWK
(*Accipiter cooperii*)

Description. Length 16 inches. Back gray-blue, reddish-streaked breast, and red eye. Short, rounded wings and long tail. Slightly larger than very similar-looking sharp-shinned hawk.

Description. Uncommon year-round resident of woodlands, including ponderosa pine, Douglas fir, and spruce-fir forests.

Remarks. Captures small birds on the wing and also hunts small mammals.

SHARP-SHINNED HAWK
(*Accipiter striatus*)

Description. Length 14 inches. Very similar to Cooper's hawk, with rounded wings, but shorter, squared tail. Reddish brown back and rusty-white barred breast. Barred tail and underwings.

Distribution. Uncommon year-round resident of ponderosa, Douglas fir, and spruce-fir forests.

Remarks. Captures small mammals and birds on the wing as it darts in and out of trees.

GOLDEN EAGLE
(Aquila chrysaetos)

Description. Length 40 inches. Body brown overall with golden-yellow head and neck. Large wings and short, broad tail. Immature golden eagles have white wing patches at base of primaries and white tail with dark terminal band.

Distribution. Fairly common year-round resident. Open country. Commonly seen soaring above timberline in the alpine zone.

Remarks. Nests on cliffs. Feeds on rabbits, marmots, and other small mammals.

Golden eagles are commonly seen soaring along cliffs and ridges in the alpine tundra regions.

RED-TAILED HAWK
(Buteo jamaicensis)

Description. Length 22 inches. Reddish brown back, creamy streaked breast. Diagnostic red tail. Dark bars near shoulders. Broad wings and short, broad tail.

Distribution. Common year-round resident. Open country, ponderosa pine forest, riparian areas.

Remarks. Screaming call is *keeer!* Soars on broad, outstretched wings. Feeds on small rodents.

NORTHERN HARRIER
(Circus cyaneus)

Description. Length 23 inches. Slender body, with long tail and broad wings. Male has grayish back and head with white underparts. Female brown with streaked, whitish underparts. White rump diagnostic.

Distribution. Uncommon year-round resident. Open-country grasslands, tundra, and wetlands.

Remarks. Often soars in fluttery manner just above the ground hunting small rodents.

PRAIRIE FALCON
(Falco mexicanus)

Description. Length 19 inches. Light brown back with streaked, creamy breast. Black "whiskers" on cheeks. Wings and tail pointed. Dark patch near shoulder on underside of outstretched wings.

Distribution. Uncommon year-round resident of open country. Commonly seen on Trail Ridge Road.

Remarks. Often hunts mammals and sometimes birds low to the ground.

Prairie falcon about to fledge. Prairie falcons nest on cliffs and, despite their name, are also found in the mountains.

AMERICAN KESTREL
(*Falco sparverius*)

Description. Length 11 inches. Smallest of the falcons. Narrow, long wings and broad tail. Reddish brown back and tail, with double black "whiskers" on cheeks. Male has blue-gray wings; female is all reddish brown.

Distribution. Common year-round resident. Open country. Common in aspen and ponderosa pine forests.

Remarks. Often hovers. Feeds on small rodents, grasshoppers, and birds. Cavity nester. Previously known as sparrow hawk.

Chickenlike Birds

These ground-nesting birds tend to walk more than fly. Young are able to walk immediately after hatching. There are seven species in the park, but only two are discussed below.

BLUE GROUSE
(Dendragapus obscurus)

Description. Length 20 inches. Males bluish gray on back, with yellowish orange comb above the eye. Females mottled brown.
Distribution. Fairly common year-round residents of woodlands, including aspen, Douglas fir, and spruce-fir forest.
Remarks. Rather tame and easily approached. Moves up to higher elevations in winter, where it feeds on the buds of spruce and fir trees.

WHITE-TAILED PTARMIGAN
(Lagopus leucurus)

Description. Length 12 inches. In summer, mottled brown with white belly. In winter, pure white plumage.
Distribution. Fairly common year-round resident of alpine tundra. Best seen along Trail Creek Road.
Remarks. Feathered feet enable it to walk on snow. Ptarmigan were eliminated from other regions by widespread domestic sheep grazing, which trampled nests and destroyed willow patches used for cover and food.

Shorebirds

Shorebirds are compact, plump birds that feed on insects along the edges of lakes and streams. Sixteen species are reported for Rocky Mountain National Park, but only three species are common enough to discuss here.

KILLDEER
(Charadrius vociferus)

Description. Length 11 inches. Brown back with white belly and breast. Double black stripes across throat and chest. Reddish brown rump seen in flight.
Distribution. Fairly common summer resident. Found along streams and wetlands.
Remarks. Feigns a broken wing to distract intruders if too close to nest.

SPOTTED SANDPIPER
(Actitis macularia)

Description. Length 8 inches. Brown back and head, with spotted white breast. Loses its spots in winter.
Distribution. Common migrant and summer resident along waterways and lakes.
Remarks. Teeters and bobs as it walks.

COMMON SNIPE
(Gallinago gallinago)

Description. Length 11 inches. Stocky bird, with short legs. Black-and-white-striped head, rusty tail, and long bill.
Distribution. Fairly common summer resident and migrant among dense vegetation along streams and wetlands.
Remarks. Rapid flight in zigzag pattern. During breeding season, male flies high and then dives suddenly, vibrating air through tail to create a loud *whooo* sound.

Doves and Pigeons

Doves and pigeons are plump, streamlined birds that are strong fliers. They typically bob their heads. Three species are reported for Rocky Mountain National Park.

BAND-TAILED PIGEON
(Columba fasciata)

Description. Length 14 inches. Purple head and breast, gray back. White stripe at base of neck.
Distribution. Uncommon summer resident, with a few remaining year-round. Brushy hillsides and ponderosa pine forests.
Remarks. Often gathers in large flocks.

ROCK DOVE
(Columba livia)

Description. Length 12 inches. The ordinary city pigeon. Some are multicolored, but most are grayish with dark head.
Distribution. Fairly common year-round resident, typically near urban areas like Estes Park.
Remarks. Introduced from Europe and typically associated with city parks, but some birds now found outside of urban environments.

MOURNING DOVE
(*Zenaida macroura*)

Description. Length 12 inches. Slim bodied with long, triangular tail.
Distribution. Uncommon in summer, with a few year-round residents. Found in grasslands and ponderosa pine forests.
Remarks. Makes a soft *woo* sound. Wings whistle when bird first takes flight.

Owls

Owls are nighttime birds of prey. All have immobile eyes, so they must turn the entire head to see to either side. Their soft feathers mean silent flight. They have exceptional hearing, allowing for capture of prey even in total darkness.

NORTHERN SAW-WHET OWL
(*Aegolius acadicus*)

Description. Length 8 inches. Chestnut brown above and streaked brown and white breast. Small, white spots on wings. Dark bill.
Distribution. Uncommon year-round resident of ponderosa pine and Douglas fir forest.
Remarks. Relatively tame. Call a high-pitched single-note whistle.

BOREAL OWL
(Aegolius funereus)

Description. Length 10 inches. Dark brown back and white streaked breast and belly. Small, white spots on wings. Pale bill.

Distribution. Rare year-round resident of old-growth spruce-fir forests.

Remarks. A northern species that is relatively rare in the Rockies.

GREAT HORNED OWL
(Bubo virginianus)

Description. Length 22 inches. Brown overall, with streaked breast. Large ears. White throat. Big, yellow eyes.

Distribution. Fairly common year-round resident. Forests and riparian woodlands.

Remarks. Call is series of three to eight hoots. Preys primarily on mammals such as rabbits and mice.

NORTHERN PYGMY OWL
(Glaucidium gnoma)

Description. Length 6 inches. Tiny, sparrow-size owl with long tail. Reddish brown back and streaked white breast. Black "eye" spot on back of neck. Lacks ear tufts.

Distribution. Uncommon year-round resident. Found in aspen, ponderosa pine, Douglas fir, and spruce-fir forests.

Remarks. Very tame. Cavity nester.

EASTERN SCREECH OWL
(Otus asio)

Description. Length 8 inches. Prominent ear tufts. Yellow eyes. Gray back and black-streaked, gray breast. White spots on shoulder.
Distribution. Uncommon year-round resident of lower-elevation ponderosa pine forest and riparian zones.
Remarks. There are two species of screech owls: eastern and western. Both are found in or near the park.

Nighthawks and Swifts

These wide-mouthed acrobatic hunters capture bugs on the wing. There are five species in the park, but only the common nighthawk is common.

COMMON NIGHTHAWK
(Chordeiles minor)

Description. Length 9 inches. Overall brownish mottled color. Wings long and pointed. Notch in tail. White wing bar.
Distribution. Common summer resident in ponderosa pine and grassland zone.
Remarks. Common in evening, when it is frequently observed as it swoops and dives, making a nasal *peent* call while capturing insects.

WHITE-THROATED SWIFT
(Aeronautes saxatalis)

Description. Length 7 inches. Long, pointed wings and short, notched tail. Black back, white underparts with black sides.
Distribution. Uncommon summer resident. Found along lower-elevation canyons and cliffs.
Remarks. Incredibly fast and agile flier.

Hummingbirds

Hummingbirds are the smallest birds. Their rapid wingbeats allow them to hover and even fly backward. They use their long bills to suck nectar from flowers. There are five species of hummingbirds reported for Rocky Mountain National Park, but only two are relatively common.

BROAD-TAILED HUMMINGBIRD
(Selasphorus platycercus)

Description. Length 4 inches. Long bill. Metallic green above in both sexes. Male has red throat, white breast and belly, with green side patch under wings. Female has speckled throat and reddish sides.

Distribution. The most common hummingbird in the park. Found in willow thickets, aspen, ponderosa pine, and Douglas fir forests.

Remarks. Wings create a loud, trilling whistle when flying.

RUFOUS HUMMINGBIRD
(Selasphorus rufus)

Description. Length 4 inches. Male has reddish brown back speckled with green, green crown, and iridescent reddish orange throat. Female has green back and whitish belly, with reddish spots on throat.

Distribution. Fairly common summer resident in aspen groves, riparian thickets, and ponderosa pine forests.

Remarks. Migrates through Colorado in July and August.

Kingfishers

Stocky, short-legged birds that dive after minnows and other fish in streams and lakes. There is only one species in Rocky Mountain National Park.

BELTED KINGFISHER
(Ceryle alcyon)

Description. Length 13 inches. Blue-gray crested head and back. Male has white underparts, with white throat and gray-blue breast band. Female has rusty underparts.
Distribution. Common year-round resident along streams and lakes.
Remarks. Has a loud, rattling call when flying.

Woodpeckers

Woodpeckers have sharp, stout bills with which they drill holes in trees. They have short legs and stiff tail feathers that assist in climbing trees. Eight species are found in Rocky Mountain National Park, but only four are discussed here.

NORTHERN FLICKER
(Colaptes auratus)

Description. Length 13 inches. Brown back with short, black horizontal bars, and creamy breast and belly with black spots. Black crescent across breast. Red mustache below eye.
Distribution. Common year-round resident. Found in aspen groves, ponderosa pine forest, and riparian areas.
Remarks. Feeds on ants. Often seen hopping on the ground.

RED-NAPED WOODPECKER
(Sphyrapicus nuchalis)

Description. Length 8 inches. Red crown and throat on black-and-white head. Yellowish breast and belly. White wing patch on blackish back and sides.
Distribution. Common summer resident of aspen groves, riparian vegetation, and ponderosa pine and spruce-fir forests.
Remarks. Formerly considered the same species as the yellow-bellied sapsucker. Drills holes in the bark of trees to obtain sap.

DOWNY WOODPECKER
(Picoides pubescens)

Description. Length 7 inches. Checkered black-and-white wings, white back and belly with black crown, and black-and-white face. Males have red spot on back of head.
Distribution. Uncommon year-round resident found in aspen groves and ponderosa pine and Douglas fir forests.
Remarks. Smallest woodpecker. Rather tame and tolerates human approach.

HAIRY WOODPECKER
(Picoides villosus)

Description. Length 9 inches. Similar to downy woodpecker but larger, with a longer bill. White back and belly, with black crown and sides. Black-and-white face. Male has red spot on the back of the neck.
Distribution. Uncommon year-round resident of riparian habitat, aspen groves, and ponderosa pine and Douglas fir forests.
Remarks. Less tolerant of people than is downy woodpecker.

Flycatchers

Flycatchers perch on trees or shrubs and dart out to capture insects on the wing. Many are drab in coloration and difficult to tell apart from one another. Thirteen flycatchers are reported for Rocky Mountain National Park, but only three are common enough to discuss here.

WESTERN WOOD-PEWEE
(Contopus sordidulus)

Description. Length 6 inches. Grayish olive above, with a dull white throat and gray belly. White wing bars.
Distribution. Common summer resident of aspen and ponderosa forests.
Remarks. Loud nasal *peer* call distinctive.

HAMMOND'S FLYCATCHER
(Empidonax hammondii)

Description. Length 5 inches. Both sexes greenish gray, with grayish head. White eye ring and two white wing bars. Chest grayish green, fading to whitish belly. Slightly notched tail.
Distribution. Fairly common summer resident of old-growth spruce-fir forests. Tends to be found at higher elevations than other flycatchers; usually the only flycatcher found in subalpine forests.
Remarks. Named for William Hammond, who collected some of the first specimens of this species.

CORDILLERAN FLYCATCHER
(Empidonax occidentalis)

Description. Length 5 inches. Both sexes have olive green upperparts, yellowish green throat, olive chest, and yellowish belly. Teardrop-shaped, white eye ring. Two white wing bars. Orange lower bill.
Distribution. Common summer resident in southern Rockies, but not elsewhere. In Rocky Mountain National Park, found among coniferous forests with deciduous component, particularly around springs and seeps.
Remarks. Formerly known as western flycatcher.

Horned Larks

Horned larks are birds of open, treeless country. Found in arctic tundra, alpine tundra, and grasslands. Tends to run rather than fly. Only one species in North America and in Rocky Mountain National Park.

HORNED LARK
(Eremophila alpestris)

Description. Length 7 inches. Male has dull brown upperparts, whitish belly and chest, with black collar across breast. Black "mustache" from eye down cheek, two black "horns" on crown, and white-edged black tail. Female has duller coloration.
Distribution. Very common summer resident of the alpine zone but moves lower in winter.
Remarks. During spring courtship flight, male flies in circles, singing brightly.

Swallows

Swallows have long, pointed wings and slender bodies. They fly with a darting motion, capturing insects on the wing. Five species of swallows are reported for Rocky Mountain National Park, but only four are likely to be observed.

TREE SWALLOW
(Tachycineta bicolor)

Description. Length 5 inches. Iridescent green-blue back and wings; white throat, breast, and belly. No white on cheek. Slightly forked tail.
Distribution. Common summer resident of and migrant in aspen and coniferous forests.
Remarks. A cavity nester. Arrives as much as a month prior to breeding, perhaps in response to the limited number of cavities available for nesting.

CLIFF SWALLOW
(Petrochelidon pyrrhonota)

Description. Length 5 inches. Blue-black upperparts, creamy belly, golden-orange rump patch, ruby red face with yellowish white patch on forehead. Square tail.
Distribution. Common summer resident and migrant, typically found near water. Nests in colonies.
Remarks. Mud nests constructed under the eaves of buildings, bridges, and natural overhangs.

BARN SWALLOW
(Hirundo rustica)

Description. Length 7 inches. Both sexes have deep blue upperparts, rust to creamy white underparts, brick red throat and face. Deeply forked tail and long, pointed wings.
Distribution. Common summer resident and migrant. Closely associated with human structures such as bridges, barns, and houses in the montane zone.
Remarks. Builds cup-shaped nests under the eaves of barns, outhouses, and other buildings.

VIOLET-GREEN SWALLOW
(Tachycineta thalassina)

Description. Length 5 inches. Both sexes iridescent greenish blue, with white underparts, cheek, and rump patch. Female slightly duller in coloration.
Distribution. Common summer resident and migrant near water, aspen groves, marshes, and riparian areas.
Remarks. Highest-flying of the swallows, often capturing insects on the wing more than 100 feet above the ground.

Jays, Crows, and Ravens

These birds are aggressive, gregarious, and intelligent. Nine species of this family are found in Rocky Mountain National Park, but only six are common enough to discuss here.

AMERICAN CROW
(Corvus brachyrhynchos)

Description. Length 21 inches. Body all black. Square tail.
Distribution. Fairly common year-round resident of a wide array of habitats, but most common in shrublands and montane forests.
Remarks. Often group together in large flocks in fall and winter. Familiar *caw* call.

COMMON RAVEN
(Corvus corax)

Description. Length 24 inches. Body all black. Robust, stout bill. Wedge-shaped tail.
Distribution. Fairly common year-round resident of all habitats from montane to alpine.
Remarks. Very intelligent. Often soars. Opportunistic feeder, taking carrion, small rodents, and birds.

STELLER'S JAY
(Cyanocitta stelleri)

Description. Length 12 inches. Body iridescent blue on belly, back, and tail, with black crested head and shoulders.
Distribution. Common year-round resident of montane and subalpine forests.
Remarks. Raucous and aggressive. Often begs for food from campers.

Clark's nutcracker.

CLARK'S NUTCRACKER
(Nucifraga columbiana)

Description. Length 12 inches. Body gray, with black wings and tail. White wing patches in flight.
Distribution. Common year-round resident of subalpine forests up to krummholz.
Remarks. Loud call. Named for William Clark of the Lewis and Clark Expedition.

GRAY JAY
(Perisoreus canadensis)

Description. Length 12 inches. Light gray overall, with white throat, forehead, cheeks, and undersides.
Distribution. Common year-round resident of coniferous forests.
Remarks. Bold and aggressive around campgrounds; known as "camp robber" for its habit of swooping in to grab food dropped on the ground. Nests earlier in the year than most birds, doing so in February when snow still covers the ground.

BLACK-BILLED MAGPIE
(Pica pica)

Description. Length 18 inches. Black head, breast, and back. White belly. Black-and-white wings. Black bill. Long, black tail.
Distribution. Common year-round resident of riparian areas and open montane forests.
Remarks. Nests are large collections of sticks. Depends on winter-killed carrion to get through the harsh winters.

Chickadees

These are small, active, perky birds that often form foraging flocks. Two chickadee species are fairly common in Rocky Mountain National Park.

BLACK-CAPPED CHICKADEE
(Parus atricapillus)

Description. Length 5 inches. Black cap and throat. Gray back and sides. Tan flanks, creamy white undersides and face.
Distribution. Fairly common year-round resident of aspen, montane, and subalpine forests.
Remarks. Song is a *chicka dee, dee, dee*. Bird is often active in the winter, particularly on warm, sunny days, when its cheerful call is a welcome sound in the forest.

MOUNTAIN CHICKADEE
(Parus gambeli)

Description. Length 5 inches. Grayish upperparts, white underparts. Black cap and throat, but with white eyebrow stripe and black stripe through eye.
Distribution. Common year-round resident of forested habitat, found at higher elevations than black capped chickadee, routinely nesting up to 10,000 feet.
Remarks. Often forms mixed foraging flocks in winter, roaming the forest in search of food. Call a raspy *chicka dee, dee, dee*.

Nuthatches

These small, short-tailed birds forage on tree trunks for insects. Three nuthatch species are found in Rocky Mountain National Park.

RED-BREASTED NUTHATCH
(Sitta canadensis)

Description. Length 4 inches. Gray back and wings, rusty underparts, with white throat. Black crown and eye stripe. Female slightly duller colors.
Distribution. Fairly common year-round resident. Typically the highest-ranging of the nuthatches, particularly common in the spruce-fir zone but also found among riparian areas and aspen groves.
Remarks. Often forages head-down on trunk of tree.

WHITE-BREASTED NUTHATCH
(Sitta carolinensis)

Description. Length 6 inches. Steel gray back, white underparts and face.
Distribution. Fairly common year-round resident of riparian forests, ponderosa pine forests, and aspen groves.
Remarks. Call sounds like a tiny tin horn.

PYGMY NUTHATCH
(Sitta pygmaea)

Description. Length 4 inches. Smallest of the nuthatches. Steel gray upperparts, dull brown cap with black eye stripe, white-buff underparts.
Distribution. Common year-round resident of ponderosa pine, Douglas fir, and aspen forests.
Remarks. Pygmy nuthatches often forage in small flocks, hopping up and down tree trunks. Will roost communally, with as many as 100 nuthatches found cuddled together in one site.

Creepers

These small birds have slender bills used to probe tree bark for insects. There is only one creeper species in Rocky Mountain National Park.

BROWN CREEPER
(Certhia americana)

Description. Length 5 inches. Brown overall, with streaked white underparts. Faint white eyebrow stripe. Long, stiff, rufous tail.
Distribution. Common year-round resident of ponderosa pine–Douglas fir forests, though has been found nesting in Rocky Mountain National Park to 11,000 feet in spruce-fir forests.
Remarks. Spirals up tree trunk while foraging, then darts to bottom of next tree and starts ascent up next trunk.

Wrens

These small, chunky birds with slightly curved bills are known for their beautiful songs. Six species of wrens are reported for Rocky Mountain National Park, but only two are likely to be observed.

CANYON WREN
(*Catherpes mexicanus*)

Description. Length 6 inches. Reddish brown overall, with white throat and breast, and tan belly. Longish bill.
Distribution. Uncommon year-round resident of shrubby, dry, rocky hillsides.
Remarks. The cascading descending song of the canyon wren is distinctive and lovely.

HOUSE WREN
(*Troglodytes aedon*)

Description. Length 5 inches. Light brown overall, with grayish underparts. Faint barring on wings and sides. Perked-up tail.
Distribution. Common in summer and during migration. Tends to be found in lower-elevation forests of aspen, ponderosa pine, Douglas fir, and riparian habitat.
Remarks. Has a bubbly song.

Dippers

These stocky, grayish birds feed in mountain streams.

AMERICAN DIPPER
(Cinclus mexicanus)

Description. Length 8 inches. Stout body slate gray overall, with slightly darker head and neck. Cocked tail.
Distribution. Common year-round resident along mountain streams.
Remarks. Feeds on aquatic insects on streambottoms. Will fly into water and walk or even "fly" with its wings underwater while foraging. Has a bubbly song.

Kinglets and Gnatcatchers

These small, active birds feed on insects. Three species may be observed in Rocky Mountain National Park, but only two are common.

RUBY-CROWNED KINGLET
(Regulus calendula)

Description. Length 4 inches. Olive-gray bird, with light yellow underparts and pale wing bars. White eye ring. Male has red crown, often not seen. Female lacks crown.
Distribution. Common in summer and during migration in aspen, ponderosa pine, Douglas fir, and spruce-fir forests.
Remarks. Nests in higher forested areas in summer, moving down to lower elevations in winter.

GOLDEN-CROWNED KINGLET
(Regulus satrapa)

Description. Length 4 inches. Grayish green body, with paler underparts and two white wing bars. White eyebrow stripe with black above it. Crown is orange-yellow in males and yellowish in females.
Distribution. Fairly common year-round resident of ponderosa pine, Douglas fir, and spruce-fir forests.
Remarks. Energetic, bouncing from twig to twig while searching for insects.

Thrushes

Thrushes are songbirds whose young typically have spotted breasts. Eleven species are recorded for Rocky Mountain National Park, but only four are common.

HERMIT THRUSH
(Catharus guttatus)

Description. Length 7 inches. Brown back, head, and wings and reddish brown tail. White underparts, with black-spotted breast.
Distribution. Fairly common summer resident of spruce-fir and Douglas fir forests.
Remarks. More often heard than seen. Beautiful, flutelike song.

TOWNSEND'S SOLITAIRE
(Myadestes townsendi)

Description. Length 8 inches. Gray body, darker wings with rusty brown wing patches. Tail blackish, with white outer tail feathers. White eye ring.
Distribution. Fairly common year-round resident of ponderosa pine forests.
Remarks. Named for John Kirk Townsend, an early naturalist who produced the first bird list for the Rocky Mountain region in 1839.

MOUNTAIN BLUEBIRD
(*Sialia currucoides*)

Description. Length 7 inches. Male has azure blue back, with slightly lighter blue underparts. Female more gray than blue, with bluish wings, rump, and tail.
Distribution. Common summer resident of aspen groves, ponderosa pine, and edges of meadows.
Remarks. A cavity nester that prefers open country such as snags at the edge of a meadow.

AMERICAN ROBIN
(*Turdus migratorius*)

Description. Length 10 inches. Dark gray back, wings, and tail, with rusty red breast and belly.
Distribution. Common year-round resident of grassland margins, ponderosa pine and aspen forests, and riparian habitat.
Remarks. Song a repeated *cheerio*.

Pipits

Pipits have long hind claws and white outer tail feathers. Two species are reported in Rocky Mountain National Park, but only one is common.

AMERICAN PIPIT
(*Anthus rubescens*)

Description. Brownish gray back, wings, and head. Lightly streaked tan breast and flanks. Tail black with white outer feathers, generally visible only in flight.
Distribution. Common summer resident of the alpine tundra.
Remarks. Nests have been found up to 14,000 feet, making it one of the highest-nesting birds in the region. Bobs tail continuously. Arrives on its breeding grounds already paired up and ready to nest, an adaptation to the short alpine summers.

Shrikes

These predatory songbirds with hooked bills sometimes impale victims on barbed-wire fence, giving rise to the common name of "butcher bird." Two species of shrikes are known in Rocky Mountain National Park, but only the northern shrike is abundant enough to discuss here.

NORTHERN SHRIKE
(Lanius excubitor)

Description. Length 11 inches. Pale gray back and head, with black wings and tail. Cream underparts. Black eye stripe. Hooked bill.
Distribution. Uncommon winter resident of grasslands and brushy hillsides.
Remarks. Genus name *Lanius* means "butcher" in Latin. Eats small rodents and birds.

Starlings

These chunky, glossy birds were imported from Europe. There is only one species in Rocky Mountain National Park.

European Starling
(Sturnus vulgaris)

Description. Length 9 inches. In spring, iridescent black overall, with yellow bill. In winter, heavily speckled with dark bill. Short, square tail.
Distribution. Fairly common year-round resident of riparian areas and aspen and ponderosa forests.
Remarks. Starlings are aggressive cavity-nesting birds that often outcompete native birds for a limited number of cavities.

Vireos

These small, chunky songbirds with short bills generally glean insects from shrubs and trees. Three species are known in Rocky Mountain National Park, but only two are relatively common.

WARBLING VIREO
(Vireo gilvus)

Description. Length 6 inches. Grayish green upperparts and whitish yellow underparts. Light eyebrow stripe.
Distribution. Common summer resident of aspen groves and ponderosa pine forests.
Remarks. Melodious song.

PLUMBEOUS VIREO
(Vireo plumbeus)

Description. Length 5 inches. Grayish head and upperparts, white underparts, two white wing bars, and dark tail. White "spectacles" frame eyes.
Distribution. Uncommon summer resident of aspen and ponderosa forests.
Remarks. Used to be known as solitary vireo.

Warblers

These small, active birds with slender bills feed mainly on insects in trees. Thirty-one species are recorded for Rocky Mountain National Park, but only six are described here.

YELLOW-RUMPED WARBLER
(Dendroica coronata)

Description. Length 5 inches. Gray with white belly, yellow throat, and yellow patches on rump, sides, and crown.
Distribution. Common summer resident and migrant. Found in riparian habitat and spruce-fir, ponderosa pine, Douglas fir, and aspen forests.
Remarks. Most abundant warbler in North America. Once called Audubon's warbler.

YELLOW WARBLER
(Dendroica petechia)

Description. Length 5 inches. Bright yellow body with greenish wings and tail. In breeding season, male has reddish streaking on breast.
Distribution. Uncommon summer resident and migrant. Found in riparian habitat and aspen groves.
Remarks. Energetic, often seen darting from branch to branch among shrubs and thickets.

TOWNSEND'S WARBLER
(Dendroica townsendi)

Description. Length 5 inches. Greenish upperparts, yellow underparts streaked with black. Two white wing bars. Male has black throat, cheek patch, and crown. Female has yellow throat and white belly.
Distribution. Uncommon migrant and summer resident of Douglas fir, spruce-fir, ponderosa pine, and aspen forests.
Remarks. Named for naturalist John Kirk Townsend. Typically forages high in conifers.

MACGILLIVRAY'S WARBLER
(Oporornis tolmiei)

Description. Length 6 inches. Grayish olive upperparts, yellow underparts, white crescents below and above eyes. Pink legs. Male has black bib and blue-gray hood. Female has brownish gray hood.
Distribution. Uncommon summer resident of riparian habitat.
Remarks. Shy and secretive, difficult to observe among the dense shrubs and thickets it prefers.

VIRGINIA'S WARBLER
(Vermivora virginiae)

Description. Length 5 inches. Grayish head, back, and wings. Yellow breast and undertail. White belly and throat.
Distribution. Uncommon summer resident of aspen, ponderosa pine, and riparian habitat.
Remarks. Often flicks its tail while feeding. Named for the wife of Army surgeon William Anderson.

WILSON'S WARBLER
(Wilsonia pusilla)

Description. Length 5 inches. Yellow underparts, greenish yellow upperparts, black bill and eyes. Male has black cap.
Distribution. Common summer resident of riparian habitat.
Remarks. Energetic bird; darts from branch to branch among streamside willows and thickets.

Tanagers

These brightly colored birds of tropical origin feed on insects and small fruits. Three species are recorded in Rocky Mountain National Park, but only one is likely to be seen.

WESTERN TANAGER
(Piranga ludoviciana)

Description. Length 7 inches. Male has golden yellow body, wing bars, and rump, with red head. Wings and tail black. Female is olive with yellowish underparts and faint wing bars.
Distribution. Uncommon summer resident of the ponderosa pine and Douglas fir forest.
Remarks. Male's voice is robinlike.

Juncos, Sparrows, Grosbeaks, Buntings, and Towhees

All of these birds have stout bills for seed eating. Twenty-six species are reported for Rocky Mountain National Park, but only nine are discussed here. (There are two groups of grosbeaks: some are associated with finches, others are listed here.)

GRAY-HEADED JUNCO
(*Junco hyemalis*)

Description. Length 7 inches. Gray head, chestnut back, and light grayish belly. White outer tail feathers distinctive when bird flies.
Distribution. Common year-round resident of ponderosa pine, Douglas fir, aspen, and spruce-fir forests.
Remarks. There are five different forms of juncos in Colorado, each quite different from the other. The gray-headed junco is the most common nester in the mountains, but the dark-eyed junco is common outside of the breeding season.

LINCOLN'S SPARROW
(*Melospiza lincolnii*)

Description. Length 6 inches. Grayish brown overall, with black streaks on back. Belly white, breast tannish with black streaks. Reddish brown crown. Grayish cheeks and eyebrows.
Distribution. Common summer resident in riparian areas, bogs, and wetlands, including those adjacent to timberline krummoltz forests.
Remarks. Secretive bird. Nesting areas are frequently flooded by late-season snowmelt.

SONG SPARROW
(*Melospiza melodia*)

Description. Length 7 inches. Streaked brown back and wings, with dark central breast spot and rufous head stripes.
Distribution. Common year-round resident in wetlands and riparian areas.
Remarks. Song sparrow has a complex and lovely song that can be heard throughout the year.

SAVANNAH SPARROW
(Passerculus sandwichensis)

Description. Length 6 inches. Brown upperparts, light breast with black streaks.
Distribution. Fairly common summer resident and migrant of open terrain such as alpine tundra, wetlands, and grasslands.
Remarks. Species *sandwichensis* named for a bay in Alaska's Aleutian Islands.

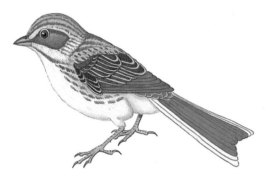

VESPER SPARROW
(Pooecetes gramineus)

Description. Length 6 inches. Tannish upperparts and slightly lighter underparts. Sides and back streaked with black. Chestnut shoulder patch.
Distribution. Fairly common migrant and summer resident of open country such as grasslands and tundra.
Remarks. The bird's Latin name means "grass lover," referring to its preferred habitat.

BREWER'S SPARROW
(Spizella breweri)

Description. Length 5 inches. Very light brown upperparts streaked with black on crown and upper back. Unstreaked buff underparts.
Distribution. Uncommon in open country, including alpine tundra, grasslands, and dry areas with shrubby vegetation.
Remarks. Named for Thomas Brewer, who studied bird behavior.

CHIPPING SPARROW
(Spizella passerina)

Description. Length 6 inches. Brown upperparts and unstreaked grayish underparts. White throat and prominent rusty brown cap. Black eye stripe and white eyebrow.
Distribution. Common migrant and summer resident in ponderosa pine forest and grasslands.
Remarks. One of the most common breeding sparrows in montane parks.

WHITE-CROWNED SPARROW
(Zonotrichia leucophrys)

Description. Length 7 inches. Brownish gray streaked back and unstreaked underparts. Whitish belly and grayish chest. Large, white crown bordered by black. White eyebrow stripe.
Distribution. Common summer resident in the stunted trees near timberline, as well as wetlands and thickets along streams.
Remarks. Song a whistling trill.

GREEN-TAILED TOWHEE
(Pipilo chlorurus)

Description. Length 7 inches. Greenish upperparts and grayish face and breast. White throat. Rufous crown.
Distribution. Common summer resident and migrant in ponderosa pine forests and dry hillsides, particularly sage-covered slopes.
Remarks. Uses both feet to scratch at ground to expose seeds and insects.

Blackbirds

These robin-size birds have sharp-pointed bills. Five species are reported for Rocky Mountain National Park, but only three are common.

RED-WINGED BLACKBIRD
(Agelaius phoeniceus)

Description. Length 10 inches. Male glossy black overall, with red shoulder patch edged in yellow. Female brown with streaked breast.
Distribution. Uncommon summer resident of wetlands and riparian areas.
Remarks. One of the earliest harbingers of spring, filling cattail marshes with loud territorial calls during breeding season.

BREWER'S BLACKBIRD
(Euphagus cyanocephalus)

Description. Length 9 inches. Male has all-black iridescent body; head sometimes appears purple in bright light. Bright yellow eyes. Female gray-brown with dark eyes.
Distribution. Uncommon migrant and summer resident of grasslands, riparian areas, and wetlands.
Remarks. Often seen around campgrounds scavenging for leftover food.

BROWN-HEADED COWBIRD
(Molothrus ater)

Description. Length 8 inches. Male glossy black with brown head. Female gray-brown all over.
Distribution. Fairly common summer resident of grasslands, riparian areas, and aspen and ponderosa pine forests.
Remarks. A nest parasite that lays its own eggs in nests of other birds, which then raise the aggressive young cowbirds, often at the expense of their own young. Cowbirds are known to parasitize 140 species of birds.

Finches, Grosbeaks, and Crossbills

These birds have stout bills for crushing and eating seeds. There are thirteen species in Rocky Mountain National Park, but only six are discussed here.

PINE SISKIN
(Carduelis pinus)

Description. Length 5 inches. Brown, streaked upperparts and lighter streaked underparts. Yellow on wings and tail.
Distribution. Common year-round in ponderosa pine, Douglas fir, and spruce-fir forests.
Remarks. Looks like a sparrow but is member of finch family.

BROWN-CAPPED ROSY FINCH
(Leucosticte australis)

Description. Length 7 inches. Brown back and breast with rosy wings and rump. Brownish crown and darker forehead. Females sometimes lack rosy plumage of males.
Distribution. Common summer resident of alpine tundra.
Remarks. There are three closely related "rosy finches," the black-capped, brown-capped, and gray-capped. They were once all treated as one species, but are now separated into three. All three are sometimes seen in Rocky Mountain National Park, but only the brown-capped is common.

CASSIN'S FINCH
(Carpodacus cassinii)

Description. Length 6 inches. Male brownish back, reddish rump, throat, and crown. Brown nape and white underparts. Female with streaked brownish back and wings with finely streaked light breast.
Distribution. Fairly common year-round resident of coniferous forests.
Remarks. Often forms large migrating flocks.

HOUSE FINCH
(Carpodacus mexicanus)

Description. Length 6 inches. Male has brown upperparts, bright red chest, streaked belly, and red eye stripe. Female brown with streaked underparts.
Distribution. Common year-round resident of ponderosa pine, aspen, and riparian habitat.
Remarks. Originally confined to the Southwest U.S., but range has expanded with civilization, and the house finch is now common over much of the United States.

RED CROSSBILL
(Loxia curvirostra)

Description. Length 7 inches. Both sexes have crossed bills. Male is brick red overall, with darker wings and tail. Female grayish brown with dark wings.
Distribution. Fairly common year-round resident in coniferous forests.
Remarks. Uses special bill to open scales on coniferous cones to extract seeds.

PINE GROSBEAK
(Pinicola enucleator)

Description. Length 10 inches. Male has rosy body, black wings and tail, and white wing bars. Female gray with brownish head and white wing bars.
Distribution. Fairly common year-round resident of coniferous forests.
Remarks. Call a distinctive *tee-wheet-tee*.

Weaver Finches

These are small, seed-eating birds of the Old World. The house sparrow, which was introduced from Europe, is the only representative in Rocky Mountain National Park.

HOUSE SPARROW
(Passer domesticus)

Description. Length 6 inches. Male has streaked brown-red back, pale underparts, gray cap, and black throat. Female similar but lacks the gray cap and black throat.
Distribution. Fairly common year-round resident near human habitation and in grasslands.
Remarks. Introduced from Europe in 1850, the house sparrow has spread across the United States, where it aggressively outcompetes native species for cavity nesting sites.

Mammals

Mammals are warm-blooded, with a body covering of hair or fur, although some species, such as whales, are hairless as adults. They breathe with lungs and feed their young with milk. Most mammals have four feet and a tail. Although there is not as large a diversity of mammal species as those of other vertebrate animal groups, such as fish, reptiles, and birds, mammals dominate many of the environments where they are found. It is theorized that mammals evolved from primitive reptilian ancestors beginning some 153 million years ago. During the early part of their evolution, mammals remained small and were a relatively obscure animal group. The extinction of the dinosaurs 65 million years ago permitted a rapid diversification of life, including among mammal groups. There are three major groups of mammals: monotremes, which lay eggs; marsupials, which rear their young in pouches; and placental mammals, which have fetuses nurtured by placentas. The placental mammals are the most advanced and successful.

Being able to maintain an internal temperature is necessary for mammals to exploit environments where cold temperatures are the norm, such as the high mountains of Rocky Mountain National Park. Hair or fur provides insulation, critical for maintaining internal temperatures, and often protective coloration. It also may play a part in behavioral signals.

One of the most distinctive features of mammals is mammary glands. All female mammals produce milk to feed their young. This may provide greater opportunities for learning and intelligence, since there is often a long dependency and intimacy between mammal mother and young not found in many other kinds of animals.

The young of mammals, like birds, can be altricial or precocial. Altricial young are born relatively helpless, requiring a long period of parental care and investment, as in humans. Precocial young, such as deer, are able to run and live away from the parents for periods of time, even immediately after birth. The longer the period of dependency, the greater the degree of learning. Bears, for example, must learn a complex array of skills and detailed knowledge of food resources over a large area. They tend to be dependent upon their mothers for several years, whereas other species are quickly weaned and on their own.

Mammals at Rocky Mountain National Park

Montane Zone
The montane zone on the eastern side of Rocky Mountain National Park lies between 7,800 and 9,500 feet and is dominated by ponderosa pine, Douglas fir, and, at higher elevations, lodgepole pine forests. There are also aspen groves, open parks, and riparian areas. Larger mammals most likely to be encountered in this zone include the mule deer, elk, and bighorn sheep. Look for elk in Horseshoe and Beaver Park, and bighorn sheep at the base of Bighorn Mountain. Predators likely to be seen include the coyote and the more secretive mountain lion and black bear. Smaller mammals of this zone include the Abert squirrel, strongly associated with ponderosa pine forests, and the red squirrel, which is at home among Douglas fir and lodgepole pine forests. Also occurring in the upper levels of the montane zone among Douglas fir and lodgepole pine forests are the snowshoe hare, ermine, marten, and southern red-backed vole. Other mammals that may be encountered in the montane zone include the Colorado and least chipmunks, small-footed myotis, badger, golden-mantled ground squirrel, deer mouse, bushy-tailed wood rat, Nuttall's cottontail, striped skunk, and meadow, long-tailed, and montane voles. Species that are more common in aspen groves include the northern pocket gopher, montane vole, and montane and masked shrews.

Subalpine Zone
The subalpine zone lies between 9,500 feet and timberline at 11,500 feet. Spruce-fir forests dominate this zone, but limber pine is sometimes found on higher dry, rocky ridges, and lodgepole pine is sometimes abundant at the interface of the montane and subalpine regions. There are also lush subalpine meadows. This is the zone of greatest snowfall, limiting

Yellow-bellied marmots are common among rockpiles in the alpine zone.

which species remain as year-round residents. Deer and elk, for instance, use this zone in summer but move to lower elevations in winter. On the west slope of the park, the long-legged moose are common in this zone year-round. Black bears roam the zone in summer but hibernate in winter. Other species found in this zone include the marten, snowshoe hare, red squirrel, ermine, long-tailed weasel, deer mouse, porcupine, masked and northern water shrews, long-tailed and southern red-backed voles, yellow-bellied marmot, Uinta and least chipmunks, and hoary and long-legged bats.

Alpine Zone

The alpine zone extends from timberline at 11,500 feet up to 14,000 feet or higher. Here rocky areas, short shrubs, and alpine meadows with cushion-type plants and other alpine vegetation dominate the landscape. The harsh winter conditions that predominate most of the year permit very few species to live year-round in this zone. Most mammals use the area only in summer or hibernate to avoid the worst winter conditions. Larger animals likely to be seen here include the elk, mule deer, and bighorn sheep. Though most elk and deer migrate to lower elevations in winter, some bighorn sheep spend the winter in the alpine, surviving on windblown ridges, where the wind keeps forage free of snow. Other species one might encounter in the alpine zone include the northern pocket gopher, pika, yellow-bellied marmot, masked and dwarf shrews, and least chipmunk.

Species Accounts

Because of their adaptations, mammals have been successful in colonizing Rocky Mountain National Park. Sixty-five species are known or suspected to live in or to have once inhabited the park. Several have been extirpated, including the wolf, grizzly bear, and bison. There is some conjecture as to whether pronghorn antelope were ever present.

Exercise caution when interpreting species descriptions. All colors, sizes, and other information are only approximate to give a general idea of the size of the animal or its coloration. Size varies among sexes and age classes. The color of animal fur is influenced by the season of the year and age. Use all descriptive terms as a relative guide, but recognize that great variability exists in nature.

Shrews

Shrews are the world's smallest mammals. They are mouselike in shape, with pointy snouts, small eyes, and tiny ears usually not visible beneath their fur. The teeth of North American shrews have pigmented, brownish tips. These tiny animals have a large surface area for their small body volume, causing a lot of heat loss. As a consequence, they must eat a tremendous amount of food. On average, they feed every three hours. Their hearts can beat over 1,000 times per minute, and a shrew without access to food for even a day will die of starvation. When startled, shrews emit a high-pitched, twittering sound. They spend most of their time in shallow tunnels in soil or runways. Five species of shrews are reported for Rocky Mountain National Park.

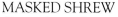

MASKED SHREW
(Sorex cinereus)

Description. Head and body 2½ inches, with 1- to 2-inch tail. Brownish gray, with long, bicolored tail that is tan on top and light brown below.
Distribution. Found in a wide variety of moist habitats, particularly coniferous forests, including spruce-fir, ponderosa pine, Douglas fir, and areas of lush vegetation like aspen groves. Also meadows and even alpine tundra.
Remarks. This shrew has the greatest distribution of any shrew in North America. Has an odoriferous secretion that discourages predators.

PYGMY SHREW
(Sorex hoyi)

Description. Head and body 2¼ to 2½ inches, with 1-inch tail. Reddish brown to gray on back fading to silvery gray on its belly. Has distinctly bicolored tail.
Distribution. Coniferous forests, boggy areas, and aspen groves.
Remarks. Wasn't known to exist in Colorado until a specimen was found in 1961. Smallest mammal in North America, weighing the same as a dime.

MONTANE SHREW
(Sorex monticolus)

Description. Head and body 3 inches, with 2-inch tail. Rust-brown above, fading to lighter belly. In winter, the fur is darker. Tail is bicolored but not distinct.
Distribution. Found in moist areas of coniferous forests, including Douglas fir, lodgepole pine, and spruce-fir.
Remarks. Until recently, was considered a subspecies of the vagrant shrew.

DWARF SHREW
(Sorex nanus)

Description. Head and body 2½ inches, with 2-inch tail. Body grayish brown, with light gray belly and indistinct bicolored tail.
Distribution. Common in coniferous forests, particularly spruce-fir forests, bogs, alpine tundra, and aspen groves. Often found in rockslides in the subalpine zone up into the alpine.
Remarks. Sometimes known as Rocky Mountain shrew.

NORTHERN WATER SHREW
(Sorex palustris)

Description. Head and body 3 inches, with 3-inch tail. Shiny blackish brown, almost iridescent, upper body with silvery belly. Tail distinctly bicolored. Stiff, whitish hairs on hind feet and slight webbing between toes.
Distribution. Along fast mountain streams and in wetlands and riparian areas between 7,000 and 11,000 feet.
Remarks. Largest of the shrews, almost the size of a mouse. Will dive underwater to feed on aquatic insects and even small fish. Traps air bubbles in soft fur, thus providing waterproofing.

Bats

Bats are the only mammals capable of flight (other animals, such as flying squirrels, just glide). Thin membranes of skin stretched across elongated "fingers" form wings. In addition, most bats have another thin membrane, known as the interfemoral membrane, between the hind limbs.

Bats exploit the nighttime niches of birds, some feeding on fruit, others drinking nectar of flowers, but most in North America feeding on night-flying insects such as moths and beetles. To locate prey in the dark and to fly without hitting obstacles, bats use echolocation, emitting ultrasonic sounds that bounce back from any object. The time and direction of this bounced sound help orient the bat.

In cold weather, bats often use torpor to maintain their body temperature. When resting, they lower their metabolism to reduce their energy losses and thus the amount of food they must consume. In Rocky Mountain National Park, with its harsh winter weather, bats deal with declining prey and cold temperatures by migrating south or hibernating, or both.

Bat numbers are declining around the world, including the United States, for a variety of reasons. Habitat loss is one problem. For instance, some bats roost under the bark or in cavities found in old-growth trees. Logging has removed so many big trees that it is jeopardizing bat populations in some areas. Another cause of population decline is the use of pesticides. As insect feeders, bats ingest these chemicals, which concentrate in their bodies with devastating results.

Despite their poor reputation among humans, bats are fascinating creatures that add much of interest to the evening and nighttime sky. Watching them flit about the heavens is one of the joys of a summertime evening. With over 850 species worldwide, bats are the second-largest group of mammals. Few surveys for bats have been conducted, and the distribution, habitat use, and abundance of species in Rocky Mountain National Park are sketchy at best. Nine species are thought to occur in the park.

BIG BROWN BAT
(Eptesicus fuscus)

Description. Length 5 inches. Dark, glossy brown on top and paler below, with black membranes. Both face and ears are darker than body.
Distribution. Ponderosa pine to spruce-fir forests and aspen groves.
Remarks. Typically fly in slow fashion but can cruise at speeds of 40 miles per hour.

SILVER-HAIRED BAT
(Lasionycteris noctivagans)

Description. Length 4 inches. Silvery white frosting on dark brown hairs. Short, black ears.
Distribution. Forested areas from ponderosa pine up to spruce-fir forest. Also frequently seen along streams and in aspen groves.
Remarks. Flies in the early evening near trees, feeding on insects. Roosts under the bark of trees.

HOARY BAT
(Lasiurus cinereus)

Description. Length 6 inches. Brownish bat with white-tipped hairs on back giving appearance of frosting. Chest brown and belly nearly white. Long, narrow wings.
Distribution. Associated with forests, spending its days in dense foliage from ponderosa pine up through spruce-fir forests.
Remarks. Largest bat in North America. Sometimes makes a high-pitched chatter that is audible to humans.

LONG-EARED MYOTIS
(Myotis evotis)

Description. Length nearly 4 inches. Pale brown upper surface and lighter under-parts. Large, nearly 1-inch-long black ears.
Distribution. Open ponderosa pine forests.
Remarks. Feeds primarily on moths and beetles.

SMALL-FOOTED MYOTIS
(Myotis leibii)

Description. Length less than 2 inches. Pale yellowish brown with almost black ears and membranes. Distinct black mask across face.
Distribution. Mountain brushlands.
Remarks. Feeds low among trees and just above brush.

LITTLE BROWN BAT
(Myotis lucifugus)

Description. Length 4 inches. Glossy brown to yellowish brown upperparts, to buffy below.
Distribution. Found in a variety of habitats, including ponderosa pine and spruce-fir forests, aspen groves, brush-lands, and along streams.
Remarks. Colonial bat that often roosts in hollow trees or buildings. Migrates south for winter and hibernates in caves.

LONG-LEGGED MYOTIS
(Myotis volans)

Description. Length to 3½ inches. Reddish brown. Short ears.
Distribution. Ponderosa pine, spruce-fir, and aspen forests.
Remarks. Moths are most common food. Roosts in crevices and hollow trees.

FRINGED MYOTIS
(Myotis thysanodes)

Description. Length 3¾ inches. Upper and lower parts of body same color, generally a yellowish brown to reddish brown. Big ears. Stiff hairs on the interfemoral membrane give rise to its common name.
Distribution. Found in western states, with Colorado the eastern edge of its range. According to range maps, should be found in Rocky Mountain National Park. Not abundant. Associated with a variety of habitats, including desert shrub and spruce-fir forests.
Remarks. Concentrates on eating beetles.

TOWNSEND'S BIG-EARED BAT
(Plecotus townsendii)

Description. Length 4 inches. Fur on back is gray, with cinnamon to dark brown tips. Similar on belly, but tips of hair are lighter. Ears are 1 to 1½ inches. Lumps by nose give rises to other common name of lumpnose bat.
Distribution. Associated with ponderosa pine and mountain brushlands.
Remarks. Tends to come out of roosts only after dark, hence not often seen.

Squirrels

The squirrel family includes marmots, ground and tree squirrels, and chipmunks. All have furry tails. All have four toes on front foot and five on the hind. All nest either in burrows or nests in trees.

YELLOW-BELLIED MARMOT
(*Marmota flaviventris*)

Description. Length 25 inches, with a 5- to 8-inch tail. Heavy body with short legs and bushy tail. Yellowish brown to reddish brown overall.
Distribution. Common in all elevations from valley bottoms to alpine, wherever there are rockslides and rockpiles for cover.
Remarks. Related to groundhogs. Marmots live in colonies and whistle when alarmed to alert other marmots of danger. They hibernate all winter.

ABERT SQUIRREL
(*Sciurus aberti aberti*)

Description. Length to 12 inches, with 8-inch bushy tail. Conspicuous tufts on ears. Two color phases: Most are dark brown or black; a light phase has grayish back, white underside, and gray tail fringed with white.
Distribution. Primarily found between 7,000 and 8,500 feet on the eastern side of the park in the ponderosa pine belt.
Remarks. These handsome squirrels are almost solely dependent on the ponderosa pine, consuming the seeds from cones, the bark of young shoots, and the terminal buds of older trees.

WYOMING GROUND SQUIRREL
(*Spermophilus elegans*)

Description. Head and body 12 inches, with 3-inch tail. Looks like a prairie dog. Drab gray color above and cinnamon belly. Tail edged with white or light tan.
Distribution. Well-drained mountain meadows, talus slopes, and forest openings between 8,000 and 11,000 feet.
Remarks. Was once considered the same species as Richardson's ground squirrel.

GOLDEN-MANTLED GROUND SQUIRREL
(*Spermophilus lateralis*)

Description. Head and body 8 inches, with 4-inch tail. Looks like a large chipmunk. Buff-colored body, rusty brown head, and whitish to buff belly. White stripe bordered by black stripe running down each side of back. No stripes on face, but white eye ring.
Distribution. Associated with a wide variety of habitats, typically meadows, rocky areas, or openings in ponderosa pine to spruce-fir forests.
Remarks. Live in colonies. Hibernate in winter. Tame and often beg for food from tourists.

Golden-mantled ground squirrel.

ROCK SQUIRREL
(Spermophilus variegatus)

Description. Head and body 11 inches, with 10-inch tail. Largest ground squirrel in Rocky Mountain National Park. Upper body is mottled grayish brown near shoulders, grading to reddish brown toward tail. Belly whitish. Tail has white edge.
Distribution. Open, rocky slopes.
Remarks. Though a ground-dwelling creature, this squirrel climbs readily and sometimes is seen in trees.

RED SQUIRREL
(Tamiasciurus hudsonicus)

Description. Head and body 11 inches, with 6-inch tail. Despite its name, most individuals have brownish rather than reddish fur on back and sides, although it tends to be redder in winter. White belly, black line along side between belly and upperparts. White eye ring.
Distribution. Common from ponderosa pine to spruce-fir forest.
Remarks. Only tree squirrel in Rocky Mountain National Park. Very aggressive and will scold with nervous chatter hikers who enter territory.

LEAST CHIPMUNK
(*Tamias minimus*)

Description. Head and body 4 inches, with 4-inch tail. Tends to carry tail straight up. Rather pale reddish to grayish brown above, with whitish belly. Back has four whitish stripes and five black stripes. Dorsal stripe continues to base of tail. Two light stripes on face.
Distribution. Found in a wide variety of habitats from ponderosa pine forests up to alpine.
Remarks. Nervous creature. Feeds on seeds, insects, and berries. Lives in an underground burrow.

COLORADO CHIPMUNK
(*Tamias quadrivittatus*)

Description. Head and body 5 inches, with 4-inch tail. Upperparts grayish, reddish wash on sides. Ears blackish in front, white behind. Dark brown side stripes.
Distribution. Open terrain and rocky areas among ponderosa pine forests and brushy hillsides. Occasionally found at higher elevations but seldom beyond the spruce-fir zone.
Remarks. Not as numerous as other chipmunk species.

UINTA CHIPMUNK
(*Tamias umbrinus*)

Description. Head and body 5 inches, with 4-inch tail. Similar to Colorado chipmunk, but dark grayish brown above fading to white on belly. Dark brown side stripes and white outer stripes.
Distribution. Associated with spruce-fir forests and meadows. Tend to be found at higher elevations than Colorado chipmunk.
Remarks. Hibernates.

Pocket Gophers

Chunky, big-headed burrowers. They have fur-lined cheek pouches, where food is stored until eaten. Eyes and ears are very small. Nearly naked, ratlike, short tail.

NORTHERN POCKET GOPHER
(Thomomys talpoides)

Description. Length 6 inches, with 3-inch tail. Grayish brown overall, black patches behind ears, and white feet. Claws on front feet.
Distribution. Found wherever soft soils are found, in meadows and forest stands up to timberline.
Remarks. Dirt cylinders snaking across top of soil after snowmelt indicate winter tunnels of northern pocket gophers under the snow.

New World Mice and Rats

Includes wood rats, voles, harvest mice, and white-footed mice. Have large eyes and ears; tails approximately same length as body.

BUSHY-TAILED WOOD RAT
(Neotoma cinerea)

Description. Length 9 inches, with 6-inch tail. Body gray-black, with white belly and feet. Long, bushy, squirrel-like tail.
Distribution. Usually associated with cliffs and caves, where it constructs nest in crevices. Has been found up to 14,000 feet in some parts of Colorado.
Remarks. Sometimes called pack rat for its habit of collecting objects. Nests are full of sticks, rocks, and bits of debris, including human throwaway pop-tops, bottle caps, and such.

MEXICAN WOOD RAT
(Neotoma mexicana)

Description. Head and body to 7 inches, with 6-inch tail. Typically gray with a reddish wash and dark hairs, with white-gray belly. Tail white to pale gray below and black above.
Distribution. Prefers dry habitat. Found among cliffs and rocky areas at lower elevations of the ponderosa pine zone and dry, shrubby hillsides.
Remarks. Tends not to build stick nests like other wood rats; rather, nest is typically shredded bark in a crevice.

ROCK MOUSE
(Peromyscus difficilis)

Description. Head and body 4 inches, with 5-inch tail. Usually brown-black above, with white to silver belly. Tail longer than head and body.
Distribution. Favors cliffs and rocky areas with big boulders and brush at lower elevations of the ponderosa pine zone.
Remarks. Seeds and fungi major part of diet.

WESTERN JUMPING MOUSE
(Zapus princeps)

Description. Head and body 4 inches, with 6-inch tail. Dark back, yellowish sides, and whitish belly. Large hind feet and long tail.
Distribution. Found in moist areas in spruce-fir forests, alpine meadows, and streamside vegetation.
Remarks. Hibernates in winter.

RED-BACKED VOLE
(*Clethrionomys gapperi*)

Description. Head and body 4 inches, with 2-inch tail. Has smaller ears and tail than do mice. Rusty red band along back, with whitish silver on belly. Tail bicolored.
Distribution. Spruce-fir forests and adjacent meadows.
Remarks. Make nests under logs, roots, and rocks.

SAGEBRUSH VOLE
(*Lagurus curtatus*)

Description. Head and body 4 inches, with 1-inch tail. Mouselike but with smaller ears and short tail. Pale gray above and silver-white below.
Distribution. Found at lower elevations among sagebrush.
Remarks. Eats the bark, seeds, and roots of sagebrush.

LONG-TAILED VOLE
(*Microtus longicaudus*)

Description. Head and body 5 inches, with 3-inch tail. Dark gray or reddish brown streaked with brown or black highlights, fading to pale gray or tan-white belly. Whitish feet. Tail bicolored. Longest tail of any vole in region.
Distribution. Found in a wide variety of habitats, including ponderosa pine, Douglas fir, lodgepole pine, and spruce-fir forests, as well as meadows, riparian areas, and aspen groves.
Remarks. Feeds on green vegetation, bark of trees and shrubs, seeds, and berries.

MONTANE VOLE
(Microtus montanus)

Description. Head and body 5 inches, with 2-inch tail. Upperparts of body grayish brown to blackish, giving it a grizzled look, with gray to white belly. Feet grayish. Difficult to distinguish from long-tailed vole.
Distribution. Found in a wide variety of habitats, including ponderosa pine, Douglas fir, lodgepole pine, spruce-fir, and aspen forests, as well as meadows and riparian areas. Its favorite habitat, how-ever, is drier meadows.
Remarks. Like lemmings in the Arctic, montane vole populations appear to cycle between highs and lows every four years.

HEATHER VOLE
(Phenacomys intermedius)

Description. Head and body 4 inches, with 1- to 2-inch tail. Body grayish with brown, silvery belly, whitish feet. Tail short, bicolored.
Distribution. Associated with a wide variety of habitats but not common. Appears to prefer meadows adjacent to spruce-fir forests above 9,000 feet and is reported for alpine areas as well.
Remarks. Unlike other voles, tends to cache food near its nest for future consumption.

MUSKRAT
(Ondatra zibethica)

Description. Head and body 14 inches, with 10-inch tail. Tail is naked, scaly, and flattened dorsally. Upperparts brown, with silvery belly. Partial webbing of hind feet.
Distribution. Wetlands and riparian areas.
Remarks. *Musk* in name refers to secretions from glands located near base of tail. Creates lodges of vegetation similar to those of beaver, but smaller.

Beaver

Large rodents, weighing up to sixty pounds. Live in water.

BEAVER
(Castor canadensis)

Description. Head and body 30 inches, with 10-inch tail. May weigh up to 60 pounds. Dark brown fur all over, except broad, flat, naked tail. Webbed feet.
Distribution. Always associated with streams and wetlands.
Remarks. Dam of sticks and conical house in pond are evidence of beaver activity. The beaver prefers aspen, alder, willow, and cottonwood. When alarmed, slaps water loudly with tail as it dives.

Beaver dams, such as this one along Hidden Valley Creek, are important for water storage and flood control.

Porcupine.

Porcupine
Dark-colored rodent with needle-like spines.

PORCUPINE
(Erethizon dorsatum)

Description. Head and body 22 inches, with 9-inch tail. Heavy body, with short legs and quills all over body.
Distribution. Found in forested areas.
Remarks. The slow-moving but quill-covered porcupine is seldom molested. A few predators, including the mountain lion, appear able to successfully capture and eat the prickly animal.

Pikas, Rabbits, and Hares

Pikas, rabbits, and hares are members of the order Lagomorpha. Though they appear related to rodents, they evolved from entirely different ancestors. Rabbits and hares look similar, with long ears and large hind feet for jumping, but they have very different life strategies. Rabbits give birth to naked, immature young whose eyes are closed. Baby hares are born completely furred, with eyes open, and are able to move within hours of birth. Rabbits and hares share a unique habit of reingesting feces to increase digestion and extraction of nutrients.

PIKA
(Ochotona princeps)

Description. Head and body 8 inches. No visible tail. Looks like a small rabbit with small, rounded ears. Grayish to tan. Makes a series of sharp squeaks when alarmed.
Distribution. Subalpine and alpine zones among rockslides and boulder fields.
Remarks. Cute animal that stores grass and other vegetation under rocks for winter food. Is active under snow all winter.

SNOWSHOE HARE
(Lepus americanus)

Description. Head and body 18 inches. Large feet. Body white in winter, brown in summer. White tail. Ears 4 inches long.
Distribution. Douglas fir and spruce-fir forests.
Remarks. Large, furry feet carry the animal easily on snow.

Snowshoe hare.

WHITE-TAILED JACKRABBIT
(Lepus townsendii)

Description. Head and body 22 inches. Ears 6 inches long. Brown in summer, with white rump and tail. All white in winter. Looks similar to snowshoe rabbit, except feet and ears are both longer.
Distribution. Open areas such as mountain parks or alpine tundra areas.
Remarks. Tends to run rapidly for long distances when frightened, often keeping to open terrain, whereas snowshoe hare will hold its place until forced to run for cover.

NUTTALL'S COTTONTAIL
(Sylvilagus nuttallii)

Description. Head and body 12 inches. Ears 2 inches long. Pale gray, with brown throat patch and white, cottony tail.
Distribution. Associated with brushy, dense vegetation, particularly sagebrush.
Remarks. Only cottontail in the park.

Dog Family

Members of the dog family have long, narrow snouts, five toes on front paws and four on hind paws. All have a strong sense of smell and are predators. One member of the dog family, the wolf, has now been extirpated from Colorado. A recent study found that Colorado could support as many as 1,200 wolves, including a few packs in Rocky Mountain National Park.

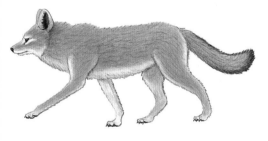

COYOTE
(Canis latrans)

Description. Head and body 35 inches, with 15-inch bushy tail. Weight 25 to 50 pounds. Gray to reddish gray, with brownish legs, feet, and ears. Throat and belly white. Sharp-pointed ears.
Distribution. Found in every major habitat type.
Remarks. Yapping bark and howl often heard in evening and early morning.

Coyote

GRAY FOX
(Urocyon cinereoargenteus)

Description. Head and body 28 inches, with 15-inch bushy tail. Weight 7 to 14 pounds. Salt-and-pepper coat, with an overall grayish tone and rusty flanks and legs. Black stripe down tail.

Distribution. Found in the lowest elevations of the ponderosa pine zone. Chiefly associated with canyons and brushy country.

Remarks. The one fox that regularly climbs trees. Eats a lot of berries, plus insects and small rodents. In winter, carrion is important.

RED FOX
(*Vulpes vulpes*)

Description. Head and body 22 inches, with 15-inch bushy tail. Reddish yellow with white belly and white-tipped tail. Legs and feet black. Erect, pointed ears. **Distribution.** Associated with aspen groves, meadows, and riparian areas. **Remarks.** The park's red foxes are part of a native mountain population found historically in the state. Red foxes on the plains have only recently invaded the state from the east. The red fox has three color phases: red, as described above; silver, which has black fur with white tips; and a cross, which is more yellowish, with a brown cross over the shoulder area. All three varieties are seen in Colorado fox populations.

Bears

Bears have stout bodies and short tails. They are plantigrade, which means they walk on the soles of their feet. The claws on the hind feet are shorter than those on the front feet. Bears are primarily omnivores, eating both plants and animals. Originally both black bears and grizzly bears lived in Rocky Mountain National Park, but the grizzly was extirpated from Colorado and is now found only in Alaska, Wyoming, Idaho, and Montana.

BLACK BEAR
(*Ursus americanus*)

Description. Head and body 6 feet. Height at shoulders 2 to 3 feet. Weight 250 to 500 pounds. Black bears come in a variety of color phases, including black, brown, cinnamon, blond, and even white (only in British Columbia). Most black bears have white chest patches.

Distribution. Most forested habitats.

Remarks. At least one estimate places the bear population in the park at thirty animals. This is not a sufficient number of individuals to maintain a viable population. These bears must be part of a larger population outside the park, and habitat in surrounding national forest lands must be preserved if the black bear is to persist into the next century.

Not all black bears are black. Some are brown, cinnamon, or even blond.

Raccoons

These medium-size animals have pointed snouts and long, bushy tails. Like bears, raccoons are plantigrade, walking flat on their feet. They are omnivorous, eating everything from fish to frogs to fruit.

RACCOON
(Procyon lotor)

Description. Head and body 25 inches, with 12-inch tail. Weight 12 to 30 pounds. Body a salt-and-pepper mix, with black mask over eyes. Bushy tail has alternating black and whitish yellow rings.
Distribution. Occurs along streams and wetlands.
Remarks. Become inactive in colder weather but do not truly hibernate.

Weasel Family

The weasel family includes a diverse group of animals, from the river otter to the wolverine. Despite this diversity, there are some shared characteristics: All members of the weasel family, except badgers, have short legs and generally thin, longish bodies. Ears are small and rounded. All have scent glands, best developed in the skunks. One member of this family, the wolverine, has not been seen in recent years and has likely been extirpated.

MARTEN
(Martes americana)

Description. Head and body 16 inches, with 8-inch, bushy tail. Similar in size and appearance to a domestic cat. Thick, generally yellowish brown to dark brown fur. Pale orange patch on throat.
Distribution. Spruce-fir and Douglas fir forests.
Remarks. Feeds on squirrels, voles, snowshoe hares, and berries. Relies upon old-growth forest and is declining in many regions due to logging.

MINK
(Mustela vison)

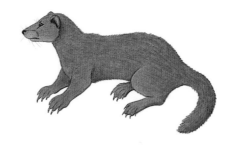

Description. Head and body 16 inches, with 9-inch tail. Weasel-shaped body, with short legs. Rich, chocolate brown overall, with small, white patch on throat. Small ears and webbed feet.
Distribution. Associated with streams, wetlands, and rivers up to 10,000 feet.
Remarks. Mink are semiaquatic. They swim well and capture trout and other fish underwater. They also prey upon frogs, birds, and anything else they can capture.

ERMINE
(Mustela erminea)

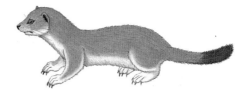

Description. Head and body 8 inches, with 3-inch tail. Thin body. Dark brown upperparts, white underparts and feet, and black tip on tail. White line on each hind leg. In winter, turns white except for black tip on tail.
Distribution. Found in all higher-elevation habitats from subalpine forests up to alpine tundra.
Remarks. Also known as short-tailed weasel. Eats mice, voles, and chipmunks.

LONG-TAILED WEASEL
(Mustela frenata)

Description. Head and body 10 inches, with 5-inch tail. Long, slender body. Brown upperparts, yellowish white underparts, and black tip on tail. In winter, all white except for black tip on tail. No white line on each hind leg, as in ermine.
Distribution. Found in every habitat except wet ones, from ponderosa pine to alpine.
Remarks. Tends to be found in more open habitat than ermine.

BADGER
(*Taxidea taxus*)

Description. Head and body 20 inches, with 5-inch tail. Weight 20 pounds. Stout body, with short legs. Gray-yellow upperparts and yellowish belly. White stripe from nose over head to shoulder blades. Feet black. Black spot in front of each ear.
Distribution. Ponderosa pine forests, sagebrush, aspen woodlands, and drier meadow areas.
Remarks. Preys on ground squirrels, pocket gophers, and other rodents. Excellent digger.

Badger.

STRIPED SKUNK
(Mephitis mephitis)

Description. Head and body 18 inches, with bushy, 10-inch tail. Weight 14 pounds. Size of domestic cat. Black with white stripe on forehead and broad, white, V-shaped stripes on either side of back.
Distribution. Found in nearly every habitat from ponderosa pine to alpine.
Remarks. Stomps feet before releasing anal gland musk. Stream is accurate up to 15 feet. Do not hibernate, but do remain dormant for extended periods of time in cold weather.

SPOTTED SKUNK
(Spilogale putorius)

Description. Head and body 13 inches, with bushy, 9-inch tail. Weight 2 to 3 pounds. Black body with white forehead, white spots under ears, and four inter-rupted white stripes along sides, back, and neck. White-tipped tail.
Distribution. Dry, rocky areas with shrubs.
Remarks. More agile than striped skunk. Climbs trees to raid bird nests.

RIVER OTTER
(Lutra canadensis)

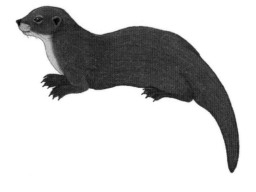

Description. Head and body 30 inches, with 16-inch tail. Long, slender body, with short legs. Dark brown overall, with a broad face like a Labrador retriever's and short ears. Webbed hind feet.
Distribution. Was extirpated from the park but was recently reintroduced into the Colorado River drainage.
Remarks. Active and curious. Very agile in water. Feeds primarily on fish. Can dive to depths of 45 feet. Dens in the banks of streams and under the roots of trees.

Cat Family

Members of the cat family have short, compact faces, with rounded ears, and retractile claws. They stalk rather than run down animals and tend to hunt in broken terrain. The lynx, a midsize cat, was once native to the area but has been extirpated from Colorado. Efforts are under way to reintroduce the species to the state.

MOUNTAIN LION
(*Felis concolor*)

Description. Head and body 54 inches, with 36-inch tail. Weight up to 200 pounds. Large, yellowish cat with long, dark-tipped tail.

Distribution. Found in a wide variety of habitats but most strongly associated with ponderosa pine forests and brushy mountainside areas.

Remarks. Other names include panther, cougar, catamount, and puma. Stalks by stealth, surprising prey, hence tends to live in more broken country or where vegetation provides some cover. Primary prey is deer and elk. One of the few animals able to capture porcupines without serious mishap.

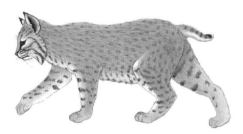

BOBCAT
(*Lynx rufus*)

Description. Head and body 25 to 30 inches, with short, 5-inch tail. Weight 20 to 30 pounds. Tawny to reddish upperparts and pale to white underparts. Short black-tipped tail.

Distribution. Found in a variety of habitats but most common in brushy or forested terrain.

Remarks. The bobcat preys upon small birds, mice, rabbits, and grouse.

Deer Family

Members of this family of large herbivores include elk, moose, and deer. Males have antlers that are shed each year. Females have no antlers.

ELK (Wapiti)
(Cervus elaphus)

Description. Height 4 to 5 feet at shoulders. Males weigh up to 1,000 pounds. Antlers may be up to 5 feet in length, with six or seven tines on a side. Buff color over most of body, with dark brown head and shoulders and yellowish rump patch.

Distribution. From ponderosa pine up through alpine. Common in Horseshoe and Beaver Parks in autumn.

Remarks. Elk were hunted to extinction in Rocky Mountain National Park by 1900. Today's elk are descendants of animals transplanted from Yellowstone National Park in 1913 and 1914. Males bugle during the September rut, but the sound is more like a high whistle than a horn.

Moose are not native to Colorado or the park but were introduced. They are common in the North Fork of the Colorado River Valley.

MOOSE
(Alces alces)

Description. Height at shoulders 6 to 7 feet. Weight up to 1,500 pounds. Large as a horse. Dark brown, almost black, although calves tend to be reddish. Males have large, palmate antlers up to 6 feet across.

Distribution. Found along the Colorado River.

Remarks. Moose are not native to Colorado but were introduced. Those along Colorado River are descendants of moose introduced into North Park. Willows are a favorite food.

MULE DEER
(Odocoileus hemionus)

Description. Height to 3 feet. Weight up to 400 pounds. Gray in winter and reddish in summer. Tail black tipped. Males have large, spreading, forked antlers. Ears large like a mule's.
Distribution. Found in a wide variety of habitats from ponderosa pine up to alpine in summer.
Remarks. Eats grass and shrubs such as sagebrush and antelope brush.

Mule deer.

Unlike members of the deer family, bighorn sheep females possess horns, although smaller and more daggerlike than the huge, curving horns of the rams.

Bovine Family

This family includes the domestic cow and the wild bison. All members of this family are herbivores. Both male and female have horns. Horns are not dropped annually like antlers.

BIGHORN SHEEP
(Ovis canadensis)

Description. Height 3 feet. Weight up to 275 pounds. Tan to brown upperparts, with lighter belly. Cream rump patch. Males possess large, curling horns. Female horns are straighter, more daggerlike.
Distribution. On steep hillsides and up into the alpine. Good place to see them is near base of Bighorn Mountain near Beaver Park.
Remarks. Bighorn sheep were once more common, even in Rocky Mountain National Park. They have suffered from diseases transmitted from domestic livestock and are gone from many areas of the West where they were once found.

HIKING GUIDE

There are over 300 miles of trails in Rocky Mountain National Park. In addition, there are fantastic opportunities for cross-country travel, particularly in the open tundra areas.

Whether you're planning a short day hike or a longer overnight jaunt, it's wise to carry along a flashlight, map, raincoat, and water. The raincoat may not seem necessary, especially on a Colorado blue sky morning, but Rocky Mountain National Park is famous for its afternoon thunderstorms, and if you wish to avoid a drenching or worse, carry the rain gear. Afternoon thunderstorms are almost predictable events in July and August, and a major concern is lightning. Always try to avoid being on a mountaintop when a storm arrives. Try to reach the top by 1 P.M. and be headed down after that. If a thunderstorm comes up, get to lower elevation fast. If you are caught out in the storm, avoid caves, overhangs, the bottoms of cliffs, and puddles of water. Try to find a flat rock or some such place to crouch on. If you have some insulation, such as a sleeping pad, place that on the ground (the electricity from lightning strikes often comes up from the ground as well as from above).

Although Rocky Mountain National Park looks wild, it is a highly controlled, regulated, landscape. If you're planning to camp overnight, you must first obtain a permit from the Park Service and pay a fee. You can't just go sleep out under the stars. Stop at a visitors center for details.

Below are brief descriptions of some of the more popular trails in the park. All distances are in round-trip (RT) miles. Trail ratings are based upon elevation gain and distance. Nearly all trails in the park are above 8,000 feet, and if you're not used to the limited oxygen of high elevations, allow more time for walking than you would at sea level. For more detailed trail descriptions, see *Hiking Rocky Mountain National Park*, by Kent and Donna Dannen.

Hikers on the Loch Vale Trail. With more than 300 miles of trails, the park has plenty of hiking opportunities.

Trails from Bear Lake Trailhead (9,475 feet)

Bear Lake Trailhead is the most popular in the park. In the summer, it's advisable to take the shuttle bus from the parking area by Glacier Basin Campground to the trailhead. A number of destinations originate from the trailhead.

Nymph Lake An easy 1-mile RT from Bear Lake Trailhead. The trail offers good views of Flattop and Hallett Peaks.

Dream Lake Moderate 2.2-mile RT from Bear Lake Trailhead. The trail winds past Nymph Lake, then ascends through small meadows with wildflowers, spruce-fir forests, and some limber pine forest to Dream Lake, with good views of Hallett Peak.

Emerald Lake Moderate 3.6-mile RT from Bear Lake Trailhead. The trail climbs past Nymph and Dream Lakes, with ever more spectacular views until you arrive at rock-ribbed Emerald Lake.

Emerald Lake is accessible from the Bear Lake Trailhead.

Bierstadt Lake Moderate 3.2-mile RT from Bear Lake Trailhead. The trail follows the top of a glacial moraine through forest to the lake.

Flattop Mountain Strenuous 8.8-mile RT from Bear Lake Trailhead. The trail switchbacks up above Dream and Emerald Lakes, eventually breaking out above timberline and providing access to the Continental Divide and views reminiscent of those in "The Sound of Music." Strong hikers can then strive to reach other peaks, such as Otis and Hallett.

Odessa Lake Moderate 8.2-mile RT from Bear Lake Trailhead. The Odessa Lake Trail branches off the Flattop Mountain Trail about 1 mile from the parking lot, climbs up over a ridge of Flattop Mountain, then levels off as it circles into the glaciated gorge that contains lovely Odessa Lake. If you have made arrangements for a pickup or a vehicle shuttle, you can continue down Fern Creek and Big Thompson River to the trail-head at Moraine Park, an 8.5-mile one-way trek.

Chapin Creek Trailhead (10,640 feet)

The trailhead is 6.4 miles up the one-way Fall River Road. Parking is limited.

Ypsilon Mountain Strenuous 7-mile RT from Chapin Creek Trailhead. From the parking area, it is a 2,874-foot climb to the top of Ypsilon Mountain. The good news is that you are already quite high in elevation when you start. The trail passes through trees for a short ways, and then climbs above timberline. It's easy to lose the trail, but you can see Ypsilon Mountain to the north of Mount Chiquita. Just set your sights on the summit and walk in that direction. It's a steep climb up tundra and rock-slides to the mountaintop, but you are rewarded with exceptional views, including the 2,000-foot drop to Spectacle Lakes. Shorter hikes following the same basic route can be made to Mount Chapin or Chiquita. Beware that most of the hike is above timberline, and exposure to afternoon lightning strikes is always a concern.

Colorado River Trailhead (9,010 feet)

This trailhead is off the Trail Ridge Road 9.6 miles north of the Grand Lake Entrance.

Lulu City Site Moderate 7.4-mile RT. Starting from the parking lot off Trail Ridge Road, this trail follows the Colorado River as it winds serenely through beautiful spruce bottoms with open flowery meadows, to

Hikers stroll through meadows along the Mount Chapin Trail.

the barely visible ruins of the mining community of Lulu City. Lulu City flourished briefly between 1881 and 1886. Moose and elk are often seen along the trail.

Fern Lake Trailhead (8,155 feet)

The Fern Lake Trailhead lies at the end of the dirt road beyond the Moraine Park Campground. Parking is limited, so try to get here early.

Fern Lake Moderate 7.6-mile RT. The trail follows the Big Thompson River 1.5 miles to the Pool, a deep, rock-ribbed plunge pool that makes for a good rest stop or picnic spot. The trail continues up the valley, then climbs up the side of the mountain toward the hanging valley containing Fern Lake. En route, you pass lovely Fern Falls. Fern Lake offers spectacular views of Mount Matterhorn and Notchtop Mountain. If you have pre-arranged a shuttle or pickup, it's possible to continue up the spectacular Odessa Gorge past Odessa Lake and take the trail to Bear Lake Trailhead. This is an 8.5-mile one-way trek from the Fern Lake Trailhead.

Fern Falls, along Fern Lake Trail.

Glacier Gorge Trailhead (9,240 feet)

Glacier Gorge is the second most popular trailhead in the park. The parking lot is located up the Bear Lake Road.

The Loch Moderate 5.4-mile RT. The Glacier Gorge Trailhead offers hikes to several spectacular destinations. The trail climbs 0.6 mile to Alberta Falls, a granite-ribbed falls. The trail winds up beyond the falls along the side of the Glacier Knobs and levels out. It continues up a truly amazing valley with magnificent vistas to The Loch, a glacier-carved lake that frames the Sharkstooth, Andrews Glacier, and other prominent features.

Mills Lake Moderate 5-mile RT. The trail to Mills Lake begins at the Glacier Gorge Trailhead and follows the same main stem as the pathway

Logs in Mills Lake.

to The Loch. At about 1.9 miles from the trailhead, you come to a junction. The right-hand trail continues to The Loch. To get to Mills Lake,
take the left-hand fork and descend to Icy Brook. After crossing the
creek, you climb up through spruce forest, where the trail levels off. It
climbs over much bare glaciated bedrock, where it's easy to lose the path.
Just head up the valley, and soon you'll arrive at Mills Lake, which frames
Longs Peak at the head of the valley. You can continue up Glacier Gorge
past marshy Jewel Lake to Black Lake, 4.7 miles from the trailhead.

Wild Basin Trailhead (8,500 feet)

To reach Wild Basin Trailhead, drive south from Estes Park 11 miles on
State Route 7 to a signed turnoff for Wild Basin. Follow this narrow road
approximately 2 miles to the trailhead.

Thunder Lake Strenuous 13.6-mile RT. From the Wild Basin Trailhead, this trail follows the North Fork of the St. Vrain River through
spruce forests to Copeland Falls, an easy 0.3 mile from the trailhead. It
continues along the stream to a bridge approximately 1.3 miles from the
trailhead. Here the trail divides. To reach Thunder Lake by the most
direct route, take the right-hand fork. If you want to view scenic Calypso
Cascades and Ouzel Falls, go across the bridge. This trail eventually loops
back to join the Thunder Lake Trail. The more direct route is basically a
moderate grade with a few switchbacks. There is one trail junction for
Lion Lakes about 1.7 miles from the Calypso Cascades trail junction. To
continue on to Thunder Lake, stay left. Eventually you reach Thunder
Lake and must descend to reach the meadow and ranger station at the
east end of the lake.

Bluebird Lake Strenuous 12-mile RT. Bluebird Lake is one of several
water storage reservoirs constructed in the park. The lake sits in a rocky
bowl below 12,716-foot Ouzel Peak. To reach the lake, start from the Wild
Basin Trailhead and continue up the North Fork of the St. Vrain River
toward Calypso Cascades. Instead of going right toward Thunder Lake,
take the left fork, cross the river on a bridge, and proceed toward Calypso
Cascades, 1.8 miles from the trailhead. After admiring the cascades, continue on another 0.9 mile on the signed trail toward Ouzel Falls, one of
the most spectacular in the park. From the falls, it's about 0.4 mile to
another trail junction. Take the left fork for the final 2.7 miles to Bluebird
Lake.

Upper end of the Thunder Lake Trail.

Longs Peak Trailhead (9,300 feet)

The Longs Peak Trailhead is 7.5 miles south of Estes Park on State Route 7. From the highway, it's another mile to the parking lot.

Longs Peak Strenuous 16-mile RT climb. At 14,255 feet, Longs Peak is the highest point in Rocky Mountain National Park, and a major climbing goal. Bear in mind that this is a long day hike that requires climbing and descending nearly 5,000 feet each way from the trailhead. Though there are no points where it's necessary to actually rock-climb, there are some narrow ledges where you could easily fall several thousand feet if you slipped. Dozens of people have died on Longs Peak.

That being said, get an early start. Most people begin the hike in darkness two hours before dawn, using flashlights to follow the well-worn trail. Chasm Lake, a spectacular glacial cirque with a sheer 2,000-foot granite wall beyond it, is 4.2 miles from the trailhead and makes a good day hike for most people. If you're climbing Longs Peak, you skip the side trip to Chasm Lake and continue on to Granite Pass, 3.7 miles from the trailhead. Once at the pass, you ascend the north ridge of Longs Peak, passing up the Boulder Fields and Keyhole to the flat, 5-acre summit.

Hikers on the Lake Verna Trail.

East Inlet Trailhead (8,391 feet)

The East Inlet Trailhead is located east of Grand Lake on State Route 278. It is 2 miles on the West Portal Road to the parking lot.

Lake Verna Strenuous 13.8-mile RT. The hike to Lake Verna begins at East Inlet Trailhead near Grand Lake. The trail goes through forest past Adams Falls and past some meadows that offer nice views of Mount Craig.

It switchbacks up through mostly lodgepole pine forest to Lone Pine Lake, about 5.5 miles from the trailhead. Fjordlike Lake Verna is another 1.4 miles beyond.

North Inlet Trailhead (8,540 feet)

The North Inlet Trailhead is off State Route 278, just beyond Grand Lake.

Lake Nanita Strenuous 22-mile RT. Some consider Lake Nanita to be the most photogenic spot in the park. But you have to earn the right to see this beauty. The trailhead is located just north of Grand Lake. The first 1.2 miles follows an old road. Continue 3.5 miles to Cascade Falls. At 7.5 miles, there is a trail junction, with the left-hand fork heading to Flattop Mountain. To reach Lake Nanita, take the right-hand fork past North Inlet Falls and up switchbacks to Lake Nokoni, 9.9 miles from the trailhead. Lake Nanita is another 1.1 miles farther.

Timber Lake Trailhead (9,000 feet)

The Timber Lake Trailhead is off the Trail Ridge Road 9.6 miles north of the Grand Lake Entrance.

Timber Lake Strenuous 9.6-mile RT. The hike begins off the Trail Ridge Road in the Colorado River Valley. From the trailhead, the trail crosses Beaver Creek and then sidehills across Jackstraw Mountain to Timber Creek. It follows above Timber Creek to a junction 3.1 miles from the trailhead. The trail occasionally switchbacks as it ascends the 1.7 miles up the mountain to Timber Lake.

Lawn Lake Trailhead (8,540 feet)

The Lawn Lake Trailhead is located in Horseshoe Park.

Lawn Lake Strenuous 12.4-mile RT. The hike to Lawn Lake in the Mummy Range is steep, passing the huge, washed-out streamed of Roaring River. The flood occurred when a dam on Lawn Lake burst, sending a wall of water down the stream. In approximately 1.3 miles, you come to the junction for the trail to Ypsilon Lake. Continue along the Roaring River up more switchbacks to the lake.

NEARBY ATTRACTIONS

Should you find Rocky Mountain National Park to be crowded, or simply want to experience some other natural areas of the Southern Rockies, you might check out the following areas, which surround the park.

National Forests

Arapaho National Forest

The 1,025,077-acre national forest is named for the Arapaho Indians, who lived and hunted in the region around the time the first white trappers entered Colorado. The forest includes the western slope of the Indian Peaks Wilderness, as well as the Arapaho National Recreation Area. The recreation area adjoins the southwestern corner of Rocky Mountain National Park and lies off U.S. Route 34. The recreation area encompasses 31,456 acres, including two large reservoirs, Shadow Mountain and Lake Granby.

Roosevelt National Forest

The 788,351-acre national forest was named for President Theodore Roosevelt. It was originally part of the Medicine Bow Forest Reserve and became the Colorado National Forest in 1910. It was renamed for President Roosevelt in 1932. The Roosevelt National Forest adjoins Rocky Mountain National Park on the east. It includes the canyons of the St. Vrain and Big Thompson Rivers. A number of wilderness areas are within the national forest, including Indian Peaks. The Peak to Peak Scenic Biway (State Route 7) is a spectacular drive, particularly in the fall when aspen are golden.

Routt National Forest

Established in 1905 as the Park Range Forest Reserve by President Theodore Roosevelt, the Routt National Forest includes 1,125,000 acres of federal lands. The forest is named for Col. John Routt, first governor of Colorado. Most of the national forest lies west of Rocky Mountain National Park, with a small portion taking in the western slope of the Never Summer Range immediately adjacent to the park. Elevations of the forest vary between 7,000 feet in the valley and 13,000 feet on the highest peaks. The Continental Divide runs through the Park Range. The Routt National Forest has several wilderness areas, including the Flat Tops, Never Summer, and Mount Zirkel. The Never Summer Range Wilderness borders Rocky Mountain National Park.

Colorado State Forest

The Colorado State Forest would more aptly be called Colorado State Clear-cut, so heavily logged is this 71,000-acre parcel of state land. The forest lies immediately west of the Roosevelt National Forest and Rawah Wilderness. Originally part of the national forest system, it passed into

Michigan Lake, in Colorado State Forest.

state hands in 1938 as part of a land exchange. The state forest includes Nokhu Crags, on the northwest border of Rocky Mountain National Park. Despite the heavy logging, the state forest provides opportunities for camping, hiking, mountain biking, and hunting.

Wilderness Areas

Indian Peaks Wilderness

This 73,391-acre wilderness lies west of Boulder, Colorado, and includes the Continental Divide from the southern border of Rocky Mountain National Park to Rollins Pass. Both the Arapaho and Roosevelt National Forests administer this wilderness. The jagged granite peaks that make up the crest of the Front Range in this area are a continuation of the mountains found in Rocky Mountain National Park. Like the park, Indian Peaks Wilderness has numerous glaciated lakes and a significant amount of alpine tundra. The area is heavily used, with 90 percent of the visitation originating on the east side. Access is off State Route 7.

Comanche Peak Wilderness

This 66,791-acre wilderness lies 40 miles west of Fort Collins. Despite its size, most of the wilderness lies less than 5 miles from a road. The wilderness lies on the northern border of Rocky Mountain National Park and encompasses the Mummy Range, a subset of the Front Range. Like the park, the area is heavily glaciated, has alpine lakes, and is home to an abundance of wildlife, including elk, bears, deer, and an occasional bighorn sheep. More than a dozen trails ply this wilderness, including the Cache la Poudre Trail, which follows the river of the same name and eventually enters Rocky Mountain National Park. The trail continues upstream along that river to its headwaters off Trail Creek Road. Access is off State Route 14.

Neota Wilderness

This 9,924-acre wilderness is 60 miles west of Fort Collins and north of Rocky Mountain National Park. It takes in the north end of the Never Summer Range. The Neota Wilderness is not as high as other adjacent areas, with elevations ranging between 10,000 and 11,800 feet. Only two trails penetrate this area. Overall the terrain is gentle.

Never Summer Wilderness

This 20,693-acre wilderness includes the west slope of the Never Summer Range, immediately west of Rocky Mountain National Park. The Continental Divide runs through this wilderness, and the Colorado River has its headwaters in the range. The glaciated volcanic peaks of this range are graced with such names as Cumulus, Nimbus, Stratus, and Cirrus. As dramatic as the scenery is, the trees are what makes this wilderness special. The Never Summer Range receives a lot of moisture for this part of the Southern Rockies, and as a result, there are 600-year-old spruce trees up to 4 feet in diameter in some of the valleys of this range.

BIRD LIST

Loons and Grebes
___ Arctic Loon
  (*Gavia arctica*)
___ Common Loon
  (*Gavia immer*)
___ Western Grebe
  (*Aechmophorus occidentalis*)
___ Horned Grebe
  (*Podiceps auritus*)
___ Red-necked Grebe
  (*Podiceps grisegena*)
___ Eared Grebe
  (*Podiceps nigricollis*)
___ Pied-billed Grebe
  (*Podilymbus podiceps*)

Pelicans, Herons, and Allies
___ American White Pelican
  (*Pelecanus erythrorhynchos*)
___ Great Blue Heron
  (*Ardea herodias*)
___ American Bittern
  (*Botaurus lentiginosus*)
___ Green-backed Heron
  (*Butorides striatus*)
___ Snowy Egret
  (*Egretta thula*)

___ Least Bittern
  (*Ixobrychus exilis*)
___ Black-crowned Night Heron
  (*Nycticorax nycticorax*)
___ White-faced Ibis
  (*Plegadis chihi*)

Swans, Geese, and Ducks
___ Tundra Swan
  (*Cygnus columbianus*)
___ Greater White-fronted Goose
  (*Anser albifrons*)
___ Canada Goose
  (*Branta canadensis*)
___ Snow Goose
  (*Chen caerulescens*)
___ Wood Duck
  (*Aix sponsa*)
___ Northern Pintail
  (*Anas acuta*)
___ American Wigeon
  (*Anas americana*)
___ Northern Shoveler
  (*Anas clypeata*)
___ Green-winged Teal
  (*Anas crecca*)

___ Cinnamon Teal
(*Anas cyanoptera*)
___ Blue-winged Teal
(*Anas discors*)
___ Mallard
(*Anas platyrhynchos*)
___ Gadwall
(*Anas strepera*)
___ Lesser Scaup
(*Aythya affinis*)
___ Redhead
(*Aythya americana*)
___ Ring-necked Duck
(*Aythya collaris*)
___ Canvasback
(*Aythya valisineria*)
___ Bufflehead
(*Bucephala albeola*)
___ Common Goldeneye
(*Bucephala clangula*)
___ Barrow's Goldeneye
(*Bucephala islandica*)
___ Oldsquaw
(*Clangula hyemalis*)
___ White-winged Scoter
(*Melanitta fusca*)
___ Common Merganser
(*Mergus merganser*)
___ Red-breasted Merganser
(*Mergus serrator*)
___ Hooded Merganser
(*Lophodytes cucullatus*)
___ Ruddy Duck
(*Oxyura jamaicensis*)

Vultures, Hawks, and Eagles
___ Turkey Vulture
(*Cathartes aura*)

___ Osprey
(*Pandion haliaetus*)
___ Cooper's Hawk
(*Accipiter cooperii*)
___ Northern Goshawk
(*Accipiter gentilis*)
___ Sharp-shinned Hawk
(*Accipiter striatus*)
___ Red-tailed Hawk
(*Buteo jamaicensis*)
___ Rough-legged Hawk
(*Buteo lagopus*)
___ Ferruginous Hawk
(*Buteo regalis*)
___ Swainson's Hawk
(*Buteo swainsoni*)
___ Northern Harrier
(*Circus cyaneus*)
___ Merlin
(*Falco columbarius*)
___ Prairie Falcon
(*Falco mexicanus*)
___ Peregrine Falcon
(*Falco peregrinus*)
___ American Kestrel
(*Falco sparverius*)
___ Golden Eagle
(*Aquila chrysaetos*)
___ Bald Eagle
(*Haliaeetus leucocephalus*)

Grouse and Ptarmigan
___ Ring-necked Pheasant
(*Phasianus colchicus*)
___ Sage Grouse
(*Centrocercus urophasianus*)
___ Blue Grouse
(*Dendragapus obscurus*)

___ White-tailed Ptarmigan
(Lagopus leucurus)
___ Wild Turkey
(Meleagris gallopavo)
___ Northern Bobwhite
(Colinus virginianus)

Rails, Coots, and Cranes
___ American Coot
(Fulica americana)
___ Common Moorhen
(Gallinula chloropus)
___ Sora
(Porzana carolina)
___ Virginia Rail
(Rallus limicola)
___ Sandhill Crane
(Grus canadensis)

Shorebirds
___ Semipalmated Plover
(Charadrius semipalmatus)
___ Killdeer
(Charadrius vociferus)
___ American Avocet
(Recurvirostra americana)
___ Spotted Sandpiper
(Actitis macularia)
___ Baird's Sandpiper
(Calidris bairdii)
___ Western Sandpiper
(Calidris mauri)
___ Least Sandpiper
(Calidris minutilla)
___ Solitary Sandpiper
(Tringa solitaria)
___ Lesser Yellowlegs
(Tringa flavipes)

___ Greater Yellowlegs
(Tringa melanoleuca)
___ Willet
(Catoptrophorus semipalmatus)
___ Common Snipe
(Gallinago gallinago)
___ Marbled Godwit
(Limosa fedoa)
___ Long-billed Curlew
(Numenius americanus)
___ Red-necked Phalarope
(Phalaropus lobatus)
___ Wilson's Phalarope
(Phalaropus tricolor)
___ Pomarine Jaeger
(Stercorarius pomarinus)
___ Herring Gull
(Larus argentatus)
___ California Gull
(Larus californicus)
___ Ring-billed Gull
(Larus delawarensis)
___ Bonaparte's Gull
(Larus philadelphia)
___ Franklin's Gull
(Larus pipixcan)
___ Black Tern
(Chlidonias niger)
___ Forster's Tern
(Sterna forsteri)

Pigeons, Doves, and Cuckoos
___ Band-tailed Pigeon
(Columba fasciata)
___ Rock Dove
(Columba livia)
___ Mourning Dove
(Zenaida macroura)

___ Yellow-billed Cuckoo
(*Coccyzus americanus*)

Owls
___ Northern Saw-whet Owl
(*Aegolius acadicus*)
___ Boreal Owl
(*Aegolius funereus*)
___ Long-eared Owl
(*Asio otus*)
___ Great Horned Owl
(*Bubo virginianus*)
___ Northern Pygmy Owl
(*Glaucidium gnoma*)
___ Eastern Screech Owl
(*Otus asio*)
___ Western Screech Owl
(*Otus kennicottii*)
___ Flammulated Owl
(*Otus flammeolus*)

Nighhawks and Swifts
___ Common Nighthawk
(*Chordeiles minor*)
___ Common Poorwill
(*Phalaenoptilus nuttallii*)
___ White-throated Swift
(*Aeronautes saxatalis*)
___ Chimney Swift
(*Chaetura pelagica*)
___ Black Swift
(*Cypseloides niger*)

Hummingbirds
___ Magnificent Hummingbird
(*Eugenes fulgens*)
___ Broad-tailed Hummingbird
(*Selasphorus platycercus*)

___ Rufous Hummingbird
(*Selasphorus rufus*)
___ Calliope Hummingbird
(*Stellula calliope*)

Kingfishers
___ Belted Kingfisher
(*Ceryle alcyon*)

Woodpeckers
___ Northern Flicker
(*Colaptes auratus*)
___ Red-naped Woodpecker
(*Sphyrapicus nuchalis*)
___ Red-headed Woodpecker
(*Melanerpes erythrocephalus*)
___ Lewis's Woodpecker
(*Melanerpes lewis*)
___ Downy Woodpecker
(*Picoides pubescens*)
___ Three-toed Woodpecker
(*Picoides tridactylus*)
___ Hairy Woodpecker
(*Picoides villosus*)
___ Williamson's Sapsucker
(*Sphyrapicus thyroideus*)
___ Yellow-bellied Sapsucker
(*Sphyrapicus varius*)

Flycatchers
___ Olive-sided Flycatcher
(*Contopus borealis*)
___ Western Wood-Pewee
(*Contopus sordidulus*)
___ Pacific-slope Flycatcher
(*Empidonax difficilis*)
___ Hammond's Flycatcher
(*Empidonax hammondii*)

___ Least Flycatcher
(Empidonax minimus)

___ Dusky Flycatcher
(Empidonax oberholseri)

___ Willow Flycatcher
(Empidonax traillii)

___ Cordilleran Flycatcher
(Empidonax occidentalis)

___ Ash-throated Flycatcher
(Myiarchus cinerascens)

___ Say's Phoebe
(Sayornis saya)

___ Eastern Kingbird
(Tyrannus tyrannus)

___ Western Kingbird
(Tyrannus verticalis)

___ Cassin's Kingbird
(Tyrannus vociferans)

Horned Larks

___ Horned Lark
(Eremophila alpestris)

Swallows

___ Tree Swallow
(Tachycineta bicolor)

___ Cliff Swallow
(Petrochelidon pyrrhonota)

___ Barn Swallow
(Hirundo rustica)

___ Purple Martin
(Progne subis)

___ Northern Rough-winged
Swallow
(Stelgidopteryx serripennis)

___ Violet-green Swallow
(Tachycineta thalassina)

Jays, Crows, and Ravens

___ Scrub Jay
(Aphelocoma coerulescens)

___ American Crow
(Corvus brachyrhynchos)

___ Common Raven
(Corvus corax)

___ Blue Jay
(Cyanocitta cristata)

___ Steller's Jay
(Cyanocitta stelleri)

___ Pinyon Jay
(Gymnorhinus cyanocephalus)

___ Clark's Nutcracker
(Nucifraga columbiana)

___ Gray Jay
(Perisoreus canadensis)

___ Black-billed Magpie
(Pica pica)

Chickadees

___ Black-capped Chickadee
(Parus atricapillus)

___ Mountain Chickadee
(Parus gambeli)

Nuthatches

___ Red-breasted Nuthatch
(Sitta canadensis)

___ White-breasted Nuthatch
(Sitta carolinensis)

___ Pygmy Nuthatch
(Sitta pygmaea)

Creepers

___ Brown Creeper
(Certhia americana)

Wrens
___ Canyon Wren
  (*Catherpes mexicanus*)
___ Rock Wren
  (*Salpinctes obsoletus*)
___ Bewick's Wren
  (*Thryomanes bewickii*)
___ House Wren
  (*Troglodytes aedon*)
___ Winter Wren
  (*Troglodytes troglodytes*)

Dippers
___ American Dipper
  (*Cinclus mexicanus*)

Kinglets and Gnatcatchers
___ Ruby-crowned Kinglet
  (*Regulus calendula*)
___ Golden-crowned Kinglet
  (*Regulus satrapa*)
___ Blue-gray Gnatcatcher
  (*Polioptila caerulea*)

Thrushes
___ Veery
  (*Catharus fuscescens*)
___ Hermit Thrush
  (*Catharus guttatus*)
___ Swainson's Thrush
  (*Catharus ustulatus*)
___ Varied Thrush
  (*Ixoreus naevius*)
___ Townsend's Solitaire
  (*Myadestes townsendi*)
___ Mountain Bluebird
  (*Sialia currucoides*)

___ Western Bluebird
  (*Sialia mexicana*)
___ Eastern Bluebird
  (*Sialia sialis*)
___ American Robin
  (*Turdus migratorius*)
___ Gray Catbird
  (*Dumetella carolinensis*)
___ Northern Mockingbird
  (*Mimus polyglottos*)

Thrashers
___ Sage Thrasher
  (*Oreoscoptes montanus*)
___ Brown Thrasher
  (*Toxostoma rufum*)

Pipits
___ American Pipit
  (*Anthus rubescens*)
___ Sprague's Pipit
  (*Anthus spragueii*)

Waxwings
___ Cedar Waxwing
  (*Bombycilla cedrorum*)
___ Bohemian Waxwing
  (*Bombycilla garrulus*)

Shrikes
___ Northern Shrike
  (*Lanius excubitor*)
___ Loggerhead Shrike
  (*Lanius ludovicianus*)

Starlings
___ European Starling
    (*Sturnus vulgaris*)

Vireos
___ Warbling Vireo
    (*Vireo gilvus*)
___ Red-eyed Vireo
    (*Vireo olivaceus*)
___ Plumbeous Vireo
    (*Vireo Plumbeous*)

Warblers
___ Black-throated Blue Warbler
    (*Dendroica caerulescens*)
___ Bay-breasted Warbler
    (*Dendroica castanea*)
___ Yellow-rumped Warbler
    (*Dendroica coronata*)
___ Grace's Warbler
    (*Dendroica graciae*)
___ Magnolia Warbler
    (*Dendroica magnolia*)
___ Black-throated Gray Warbler
    (*Dendroica nigrescens*)
___ Palm Warbler
    (*Dendroica palmarum*)
___ Chestnut-sided Warbler
    (*Dendroica pensylvanica*)
___ Yellow Warbler
    (*Dendroica petechia*)
___ Townsend's Warbler
    (*Dendroica townsendi*)
___ Black-throated Green Warbler
    (*Dendroica virens*)
___ Common Yellowthroat
    (*Geothlypis trichas*)

___ Worm-eating Warbler
    (*Helmitheros vermivorus*)
___ Yellow-breasted Chat
    (*Icteria virens*)
___ Black-and-white Warbler
    (*Mniotilta varia*)
___ Connecticut Warbler
    (*Oporornis agilis*)
___ MacGillivray's Warbler
    (*Oporornis tolmiei*)
___ Northern Parula
    (*Parula americana*)
___ Ovenbird
    (*Seiurus aurocapillus*)
___ Northern Waterthrush
    (*Seiurus noveboracensis*)
___ American Redstart
    (*Setophaga ruticilla*)
___ Orange-crowned Warbler
    (*Vermivora celata*)
___ Tennessee Warbler
    (*Vermivora peregrina*)
___ Nashville Warbler
    (*Vermivora ruficapilla*)
___ Virginia's Warbler
    (*Vermivora virginiae*)
___ Hooded Warbler
    (*Wilsonia citrina*)
___ Wilson's Warbler
    (*Wilsonia pusilla*)

Tanagers
___ Hepatic Tanager
    (*Piranga flava*)
___ Western Tanager
    (*Piranga ludoviciana*)
___ Scarlet Tanager
    (*Piranga olivacea*)

Juncos, Sparrows, Grosbeaks, Buntings, and Towhees

___ Blue Grosbeak
(*Guiraca caerulea*)
___ Lazuli Bunting
(*Passerina amoena*)
___ Rose-breasted Grosbeak
(*Pheucticus ludovicianus*)
___ Black-headed Grosbeak
(*Pheucticus melanocephalus*)
___ Lark Bunting
(*Calamospiza melanocorys*)
___ Dark-eyed Junco
(*Junco hyemalis*)
___ Sage Sparrow
(*Amphispiza belli*)
___ Lark Sparrow
(*Chondestes grammacus*)
___ Lincoln's Sparrow
(*Melospiza lincolnii*)
___ Song Sparrow
(*Melospiza melodia*)
___ Savannah Sparrow
(*Passerculus sandwichensis*)
___ Fox Sparrow
(*Passerella iliaca*)
___ Vesper Sparrow
(*Pooecetes gramineus*)
___ American Tree Sparrow
(*Spizella arborea*)
___ Brewer's Sparrow
(*Spizella breweri*)
___ Clay-colored Sparrow
(*Spizella pallida*)
___ Chipping Sparrow
(*Spizella passerina*)
___ White-throated Sparrow
(*Zonotrichia albicollis*)

___ White-crowned Sparrow
(*Zonotrichia leucophrys*)
___ Harris's Sparrow
(*Zonotrichia querula*)
___ Green-tailed Towhee
(*Pipilo chlorurus*)
___ Rufous-sided Towhee
(*Pipilo erythrophthalmus*)

Blackbirds, Meadowlarks, and Orioles

___ Red-winged Blackbird
(*Agelaius phoeniceus*)
___ Rusty Blackbird
(*Euphagus carolinus*)
___ Brewer's Blackbird
(*Euphagus cyanocephalus*)
___ Yellow-headed Blackbird
(*Xanthocephalus xantho-cephalus*)
___ Bobolink
(*Dolichonyx oryzivorus*)
___ Bullock's Oriole
(*Icterus bullockii*)
___ Brown-headed Cowbird
(*Molothrus ater*)
___ Common Grackle
(*Quiscalus quiscula*)
___ Western Meadowlark
(*Sturnella neglecta*)

Finches, Grosbeaks, and Crossbills

___ Common Redpoll
(*Carduelis flammea*)
___ Pine Siskin
(*Carduelis pinus*)

___ Brown-capped Rosy Finch
(*Leucosticte australis*)

___ Lesser Goldfinch
(*Carduelis psaltria*)

___ American Goldfinch
(*Carduelis tristis*)

___ Cassin's Finch
(*Carpodacus cassinii*)

___ House Finch
(*Carpodacus mexicanus*)

___ Evening Grosbeak
(*Coccothraustes vespertina*)

___ Pine Grosbeak
(*Pinicola enucleator*)

___ Red Crossbill
(*Loxia curvirostra*)

___ White-winged Crossbill
(*Loxia leucoptera*)

Weaver Finches

___ House Sparrow
(*Passer domesticus*)

INDEX

Page numbers in italics indicate illustrations.